The Sheba Anointing

Dedication

This book is dedicated to every woman who has ever felt the whispers of God's calling on her life, to every woman who has dared to dream beyond the confines of societal expectations, and to every woman who is ready to rise to her full potential in Christ. May these words ignite a fire within your heart, a fire that will blaze with the unshakable truth of your divine destiny.

In Honor of the Lord Jesus Christ
And The Ladies of Sheba International Churches (The Daughters of Zion)

Preface

In the tapestry of life, there are threads of purpose woven into the very fabric of our being. These threads, often hidden and obscured, are the threads of our destinies, the divine blueprints for our lives. As a prophetic speaker and writer, I have dedicated my life to helping others unravel these hidden threads and embrace the extraordinary journey that awaits them.

This book is a testament to that commitment, a culmination of years of listening to the whispers of the Holy Spirit, and witnessing the transformative power of God's revelation in the lives of women. It's a call to action, a clarion call for women to awaken to their true identity, to shed the shackles of fear and doubt, and to step into the fullness of God's plan for their lives.

Introduction

In this book, you will discover the way to obtain the Sheba anointing!!!

Sisters, gather around! The winds of change are blowing, and a new era of revelation is dawning for women of faith. God is awakening a generation of women who are ready to rise and claim their rightful place in His kingdom.

This book is an invitation to embark on a journey of discovery. A journey that will lead you deeper into the secret place of God's presence, where you'll encounter His transformative power and unlock the hidden treasures of your destiny.

Within these pages, you will find a powerful message of freedom, a message that resonates with the deepest yearnings of your soul. You will learn to discern the enemy's tactics and navigate the complexities of life with God's wisdom as your guide. You will be empowered to write your story, to pen your own prophetic words, and to leave a legacy of faith that will impact generations to come.

But this is not just a book to read; it is a call to action, a call to rise and embrace the extraordinary destiny that God has prepared for you. Are you ready to step into the fullness of your calling? Are you ready to unleash the power that resides within you?

If so, then let us journey together, hand in hand, as we navigate the path to awakening and embrace the glorious tapestry of your destiny image.

The Catalyst for Revelation

The air was thick with the weight of secrets, a suffocating blanket of unspoken truths that pressed down on me. As I lay in the depths of slumber, a dream unfolded before my eyes, a vivid tapestry of images and emotions that would forever alter the course of my spiritual journey. It was a dream that awakened within me a profound sense of urgency, a call for women to rise and reclaim there true of identity as a woman of God.

In the dream, I found myself amidst a bustling marketplace, throngs of people jostling for position, their faces a blur of anonymity. Yet, amidst the chaos, I sensed a chilling presence, a dark shadow lurking at the edges of my perception. It was a presence that whispered deceit, a voice that sought to ensnare and silence.

The shadow took the form of a formidable, imposing figure, shrouded in darkness, its features obscured by a veil of mystery. As I approached, I felt a sudden wave of fear wash over me, a primal instinct to flee that urged me to turn back. But a stronger force within me compelled me to press forward, to confront the unknown.

The figure's voice boomed through the marketplace, its words a chilling echo of ancient lies. "Women," it declared, its voice dripping with malice, "you are weak, insignificant, destined to remain in the shadows. Your place is in the home, subservient to men, your voices stifled, your dreams crushed."

A chorus of voices rose from the crowd, a symphony of agreement that echoed the figure's words. Women, their faces etched with fear and resignation, seemed to accept their fate as a matter of course. The scene was a heart-wrenching reflection of the insidious whispers of the enemy, a tapestry woven with threads of self-doubt, insecurity, and fear.

But something within THE DAUGHTERS OF ZION refused to submit. As the figure continued to spew its venomous words, I felt a surge of defiance welling up within me, a fierce determination to break free from the chains of its lies. I looked around at the women, their eyes reflecting the fear and despair that gripped their hearts, and a deep well of compassion flowed through me. I knew I could not stand idly by and let them be silenced.

Suddenly, a light pierced through the darkness, a brilliant beam of golden light that enveloped the entire marketplace. The shadow recoiled, its presence shrinking in the face of the divine. And then, I saw Her. A radiant figure, her face aglow with love and compassion, stood before me. She was the embodiment of grace and strength, her eyes filled with unwavering purpose.

She was the embodiment of the Divine Shekinah, the very essence of God's power and love, radiating a warmth that dispelled the fear and despair that had shrouded the marketplace. She spoke in a voice that resonated within the very core of my being, a voice that whispered truth and hope.

"Women," she declared, her voice a symphony of liberation, "you are not weak, but strong. You are not insignificant, but valuable. You are not destined to remain in the shadows, but called to shine your light on the world."

The marketplace seemed to gasp as her words washed over them, a wave of revelation that shattered the chains of their self-imposed limitations. The women, their faces now radiating a newfound hope, looked at each other with a sense of shared purpose. The weight of the shadow lifted, replaced by a radiant light that illuminated their hearts and minds.

As the dream faded, I woke up with a sense of urgency, a burning desire to share the truth I had witnessed. It was a truth that had been whispered through the ages, a truth that had been suppressed, a truth that was now ready to be unleashed.

The dream had been a catalyst, a spark that ignited a fire within my soul, a divine revelation that shattered the walls of my own self-imposed limitations. Know that you waare not merely a woman, but a vessel of God's power, a WARRIOR QUEEN Rev 12:1 called to rise and reclaim her destiny.

This revelation was not merely a personal awakening, but a call to action, a mandate to share the truth with women. I realized that the enemy's attempts to silence and constrict women were not merely an isolated attack, but a systematic strategy to keep them bound in fear and despair. The enemy knew the power that resided within women, and it sought to suppress it at all costs.

Are you determined to be a part of this movement? to join the chorus of voices that would rise up and declare the truth, it was time to break free from the chains of societal expectations, the whispers of doubt, and the fear that had been imposed upon us.

The dream had unveiled a tapestry of destiny, a divine blueprint that illuminated the true nature of women's calling.

It was a calling that transcended societal norms, a calling that emanated from the very heart of God.

And I knew, with a certainty that defied all reason, that the enemy would not win. dughters of Zion are not destined to be silenced, but to rise and claim there place as warriors of the faith, daughters of the Most High, chosen vessels to bring forth the light of God's truth.

As I began to explore the depths of this revelation, a profound sense of gratitude washed over me. I had been given a glimpse into the divine, a vision of the boundless potential that resided within every woman. It was a vision that filled me with a sense of awe and wonder, a sense of hope that could not be extinguished.

The journey ahead would not be easy. There would be challenges, setbacks, and moments of doubt. But you are no longer alone. The dream had awakened a community of sisters, a united force of women who were ready to rise and claim their rightful place in the kingdom of God.

It was time to unleash the power that resided within them, to break free from the chains that had bound them, and to step into there own destiny as warriors of the faith. The enemy may have sought to silence us, but they would rise with a roar, a chorus of voices that would shake the very foundations of darkness.

The tapestry of destiny was unfolding, and they, the women of God, were at the heart of it. They are the vessels of his power, the carriers of his light, the voices that would proclaim his truth to the world. And as we stepped into our destiny, they would not only change there own lives, but transform the world around them, one radiant soul at a time.

Unveiling the Divine Blueprint

The dream was a kaleidoscope of images, a vibrant tapestry woven with threads of both beauty and darkness. I found myself standing on a mountaintop, overlooking a vast, sprawling landscape. The air was crisp and clean, the sky a brilliant azure canvas. But as I gazed out at the breathtaking vista, a chilling wind swept through the valley below, whispering tales of oppression and captivity.

In the distance, I saw a multitude of women, their faces etched with sorrow and despair. Chains bound their limbs, heavy and unforgiving. They were trapped, their voices silenced, their spirits crushed under the weight of societal expectations and spiritual oppression. Their eyes, filled with longing, mirrored a deep yearning for freedom, for the restoration of their God-given identity.

As the wind howled, a voice, deep and resonant, thundered through the valley. It was the voice of the enemy, a voice that sought to diminish, to control, to confine. "Silence them," the voice boomed, "keep them bound. Their power is a threat. Their potential, a danger."

But then, amidst the darkness, a ray of light pierced the gloom. A voice, gentle yet powerful, rose above the din of oppression. It was the voice of the Lord, a voice that resonated with love, with hope, with unshakable truth.

"They are my daughters," the voice declared, "My chosen ones. Their power is not a threat, but a force for good. Their potential is not a danger, but a promise. I will release them. I will set them free."

The chains began to loosen, their shackles falling away one by one. The women, their faces now alight with hope, began to rise. They stretched their arms, reaching towards the heavens, their voices, once muffled and silent, now filled with newfound strength and determination.

As I witnessed this breathtaking transformation, I realized that this dream was not simply a vision, but a revelation, a glimpse into the unfolding of God's purpose for women. It was a message whispered into the heart of my spirit, a blueprint for liberation, a declaration of their inherent power and purpose.

In the heart of that dream, I received a profound understanding of the enemy's tactics. He wanted to silence women, to bind them with chains of doubt, fear, and insecurity. He wanted to keep them trapped in a world of limitations, where their voices were muted, and their potential remained untapped.

But God, in his infinite wisdom and mercy, had a different plan. He had designed women for greatness, for power, for influence. He had endowed them with unique gifts and talents, with a spirit that could soar beyond any earthly constraints. He had called them to be his vessels, his instruments of transformation, his beacons of light in a world desperately in need of his love.

The enemy's attempts to silence women were not new. Throughout history, he had sought to undermine their strength, to diminish their value, to rob them of their God-given authority. But the Lord, in his unwavering love and faithfulness, had always been present, working behind the scenes, weaving a tapestry of hope and restoration.

In this dream, I saw the enemy's defeat. I saw the chains of oppression broken, the chains of silence shattered. I saw the women of God rise, empowered, free, and ready to fulfill their destiny. This dream was a testament to the truth that the enemy's schemes will never prevail over the Lord's sovereign will.

The message was clear: God's plan for women was not one of suppression but of liberation. He had created them to be strong, courageous, and influential, destined to impact the world with their unique gifts and talents. Their voices, once silenced, were now destined to rise above the din of the world, carrying a message of hope, healing, and transformation.

And I knew, deep within my spirit, that this message was not just for some, but for every woman who dared to dream, to hope, to believe in the power of God's grace and the transformative power of his love.

This dream, this revelation, was a call to action, an invitation to step out of the shadows of fear and into the radiant light of God's purpose. It was a call to embrace our God-given identity, to break free from the chains of limitations, and to rise in our full potential, wielding the power and authority they have been granted through Christ.

The whispers of truth, echoing through the valleys of there hearts, were a symphony of freedom, a melody of hope, a chorus of liberation. They were a testament to the Lord's unwavering love for his daughters, a testament to the power that resides within every woman who dares to believe in the truth of his Word.

This was the beginning of there journey. It was the moment they would step out of the shadows and into the radiant light of our true identity, the moment the veil would claim there birthright as daughters of the Most High God, the moment they would rise to fulfill there destiny, the moment they would unleash the power that lies dormant within.

The dream was a catalyst, a spark that ignited a fire within, a fire that would burn brightly, dispelling the darkness and illuminating the path ahead. It was a call to action, a challenge to embrace a ladies God-given purpose, a call to rise and shine, to unleash the power that lies dormant within them, to break free from the chains of limitation and step into the fullness of there destiny.

You are women of God, created for greatness, called to impact the world with your unique gifts and talents. you are vessels of transformation, instruments of healing, beacons of light in a world desperately in need of God's love.

The time has come to rise, to step into the power, to embrace destiny, you forward to fulfill the purpose for which you were created. The whispers of truth are calling forward, urging you to unleash the power within. Answer the call, embrace the freedom, and step into the fullness of your destiny.

The Lords Decree of Liberation

The dream had been a whirlwind of emotions, a kaleidoscope of images that had left me breathless and bewildered. I found myself standing at the precipice of a vast, ethereal realm, a landscape painted in hues of celestial gold and shimmering silver. As I gazed upon this otherworldly panorama, I felt a presence beside me, a gentle, yet profound energy that enveloped me in a comforting embrace.

It was then that I saw them – countless women, their faces etched with a mixture of sorrow and longing. They were bound by invisible chains, their spirits tethered to the earth, their voices silenced by an unseen force. Their eyes, once filled with hope and fire, now held a flicker of despair.

As I watched, a deep, abiding sorrow filled my heart. The sight of these women, once vibrant and free, now bound and constrained, ignited a fire within me, a burning desire to break the chains that held them captive.

The dream wasn't just a fleeting vision; it was a divine revelation, a window into the spiritual realm, exposing the enemy's relentless attempts to silence and enslave women. It was a stark reminder of the battle that raged unseen, a battle for the hearts and minds of women, a battle for their very destiny.

The enemy, with his cunning and deceptive tactics, sought to bind women in chains of fear, doubt, and self-doubt. He whispered lies into their ears, painting a picture of inadequacy and insignificance, fueling a sense of powerlessness that kept them chained to their perceived limitations.

But the Lord, in his infinite love and compassion, had a different plan. He saw the chains, the shackles that bound women, and he declared their liberation. He had woven a tapestry of destiny, a masterpiece of love and grace, intricately designed to set women free from the enemy's clutches.

The Lord's decree of liberation wasn't just an abstract concept; it was a tangible reality, a promise whispered on the wind, a beacon of hope shining through the darkest of nights. It was a call to rise, a clarion call to break free from the chains that had bound them for far too long.

The enemy's schemes, though formidable, couldn't stand against the Lord's unwavering power. He was unveiling a new era for women, an era of awakening, an era of liberation. He was empowering women to rise above their limitations, to step into their God-given identity and fulfill their destined purpose.

This liberation wasn't about mere physical freedom; it was a liberation of the soul, a liberation of the spirit, a liberation of the mind. It was a liberation from the shackles of fear, the shackles of doubt, the shackles of societal expectations. It was a liberation that would empower women to walk in their God-given authority, to live with confidence and boldness, to step into their divine calling.

The Lord's decree of liberation wasn't a passive declaration; it was a call to action. It was a call for women to step into their power, to embrace their inherent strength, to unleash the warrior spirit that resided within them. It was a call to take back their narrative, to rewrite the story that had been forced upon them, to reclaim their voice, their identity, their destiny.

The enemy's tactics, though cunning, were ultimately futile. His attempts to silence and constrict women were destined to fail. The Lord, in his unwavering love and faithfulness, had a greater purpose. He was setting in motion a symphony of liberation, a chorus of empowered voices rising in unison, a wave of divine intervention that would sweep away the shackles of the past and usher in an era of unprecedented freedom.

The dream that had sparked this revelation was a catalyst for a spiritual awakening. It was a reminder that the battle for women's hearts and minds was real, a battle that would be fought on spiritual ground, a battle that required an unwavering faith, an unwavering belief in the power of God's decree.

The dream served as a wake-up call, a call to awaken to the truth, to unveil the enemy's tactics and recognize his relentless efforts to silence and subdue. It was a call to discern his schemes, to pierce through the veil of deception and see the truth with God-given clarity.

This awakening was not just about recognizing the enemy's tactics; it was about recognizing the power that resided within. It was about embracing the inherent strength and resilience that God had woven into the very fabric of women's being. It was about awakening to the divine potential that lay dormant, waiting to be unleashed.

The enemy sought to bind women with chains of fear, but the Lord offered a path of freedom, a path of empowerment, a path of true liberation. He was unveiling a new era for women, an era where their voices would resonate with power, their hearts would overflow with courage, and their spirits would soar with the wings of faith.

The journey of liberation wasn't a sprint; it was a marathon, a path that required unwavering faith, unwavering commitment, and an unwavering belief in God's promises. It was a path that would lead to a transformation of the soul, a transformation of the mind, a transformation of the very essence of who they were created to be.

This journey of liberation, this unveiling of destiny, was a divine call to rise, a call to embrace the power that resided within, a call to rewrite the narrative, a call to step into their God-given identity and claim their rightful place in the tapestry of creation. It was a call to break the chains of the past and step into the radiant light of their future, a future filled with purpose, power, and the unwavering presence of the Almighty.

Rising to Our GodGiven Potential

The dream, like a beacon in the night, had shown me a glimpse of the enemy's agenda—a dark scheme to silence and constrict women, to deny them their God-given power and purpose. It was a chilling vision, a reminder of the battles fought in the spiritual realm, a battle for the hearts and minds of women. But amidst the shadows, a light emerged—a divine decree of liberation, a whispered promise of freedom in Christ.

I saw women, their wings clipped, their voices hushed, their potential stifled. They were caged by societal expectations, bound by cultural norms, trapped in a web of self-doubt and fear. But then, as the dream unfolded, I witnessed a shift, a change in the atmosphere. The chains began to loosen, the shackles to break, and the voices of women began to rise. They were awakening to their true identities, embracing their God-given power, and stepping into their destinies.

The dream wasn't simply a vision of the past or a snapshot of the present; it was a prophetic glimpse into the future, a foreshadowing of a glorious awakening—a time when women would rise in their full potential, breaking free from the constraints of the enemy and claiming their rightful place in the kingdom of God.

This awakening wasn't solely about external liberation; it was about an internal revolution, a transformation of hearts and minds. It was about women recognizing their inherent strength and resilience, embracing their individuality, and stepping into their God-given roles with boldness and confidence.

But this journey wouldn't be easy. The enemy would continue his relentless attempts to hinder their progress, using tactics of fear, doubt, and manipulation. He would whisper lies, plant seeds of insecurity, and attempt to convince them that they were not worthy, not capable, not enough. He would try to keep them trapped in a cycle of self-doubt, afraid to step out and claim their rightful inheritance.

Yet, in the midst of the enemy's assaults, there would be an unwavering light, a divine beacon guiding women towards their true destinies. It would be a call to rise above the noise, to silence the lies, and to embrace the truth of who they were created to be—powerful, influential, and deeply loved by God.

This call to rise, to embrace their destinies, would come from within, a whisper from the Spirit, a gentle nudge from the heart. It would be a call to step into their God-given identities, to reclaim their voices, and to walk boldly in their purpose.

This wasn't a call to seek power over others; it was a call to embrace their own power, a power that flowed from the divine source, a power that was intended to transform their lives and impact their world. It was a power that could heal brokenness, mend relationships, and bring hope to the hopeless.

But embracing this power wouldn't come without a cost. It would require surrender, a willingness to let go of the control they had clung to, a willingness to trust God with their lives, their dreams, and their futures. It would mean stepping out of their comfort zones, embracing the unknown, and walking by faith, not by sight.

And as they embarked on this journey of faith and purpose, they would discover a profound truth: they were not alone. They were part of a sisterhood, a community of women who shared their struggles and triumphs, their joys and sorrows. They were united by their faith, their purpose, and their unwavering belief in the power of God.

This journey of awakening and liberation wasn't a destination; it was a lifelong process, a continuous unfolding of their destinies. It was a journey marked by both victories and setbacks, triumphs and failures. But through it all, they would learn to trust God's faithfulness, His unwavering love, and His unwavering plan for their lives.

The dream had shown me a glimpse of this future, a world where women, empowered by God's love and guided by His Spirit, would rise to their full potential, transforming themselves and impacting their world. It was a vision of a future that was already unfolding, a future that was filled with hope, possibility, and the unwavering love of a God who had created them for greatness.

This journey of awakening and liberation wasn't just about women; it was about the world they were destined to influence. It was about a world that needed their unique voices, their compassionate hearts, and their unwavering faith. It was about a world that needed them to rise and shine their light, to illuminate the darkness, and to show the world the power of God's love.

This was a call to rise—a call to embrace the divine blueprint, to walk in the power of God, and to live out their true destinies, regardless of the challenges they faced. It was a call to awaken, to believe, and to rise, leaving a legacy of faith, purpose, and impact that would resonate for generations to come.

This was the call of the future, a call for women to rise and embrace the God-given power that resided within them. It was a call to rise and fulfill their destinies, to transform their own lives and impact the world around them. It was a call to rise and shine their light, illuminating the world with the love and power of God.

And as they embraced this call, they would discover that their true power lay not in their own strength, but in their connection to the divine source, in their unwavering faith, and in their unwavering belief in the God who had called them to rise.

Unveiling the Power Within

Sisters, let's delve into the heart of this symphony of strength, the power that resides within each and every one of you As you journey into this revelation, envision a tapestry woven with threads of resilience, courage, and divine purpose, each strand representing the unique strength that God has bestowed upon you.

Our lives are not merely a series of events; they are a magnificent orchestration, a symphony of purpose, where each note, each experience, contributes to a harmonious masterpiece. The enemy, with his deceitful whispers, seeks to dim the brightness of our inherent power, but God, in His infinite grace, has a different plan. He whispers to your hearts, "Rise! Embrace your strength! You are fearfully and wonderfully made."

Imagine the sheer power of a woman's heart, beating with the rhythm of faith, resilience, and love. Within her, there is a wellspring of strength, a reservoir of courage that defies the constraints of the world. This isn't a mere platitude; it's a testament to the divine blueprint that God has inscribed upon your very being.

We see this strength embodied in countless women throughout history - women who faced insurmountable odds, who championed the cause of justice, who defied societal norms, who dared to dream and rise above limitations. Think of the women in the Bible, like Esther, who risked her life to save her people; Ruth, who demonstrated unwavering loyalty and love; Deborah, who led with unwavering courage, and countless others. Their stories are a testament to the incredible strength and resilience that resides within the heart of every woman.

you are daughters of the King, carrying within you the essence of His divine nature. Our strength isn't derived from outward appearances or worldly achievements; it is rooted in your connection with God, in the unwavering love and support He provides. It is a strength that can withstand any storm, a resilience that surpasses any trial.

This inner power is not a gift that is bestowed upon you only in moments of crisis; it's a constant companion, a steadfast presence that guides you through every step of your journey. It empowers you to face your fears, overcome obstacles, and pursue your God-given destinies with unwavering conviction.

The strength within you isn't merely a physical or mental attribute; it is a spiritual force, fueled by the indwelling presence of the Holy Spirit. It is the power of God, working through us, enabling you to accomplish feats beyond your own abilities. It is the ability to love unconditionally, to forgive freely, to stand for truth, and to speak with boldness.

This strength, this resilience, this divine power, is not something we you to earn or acquire; it is yours by birthright, a gift from your Heavenly Father. It is an inheritance that is waiting to be unlocked, a treasure waiting to be discovered.
This is not a mere call to action; it is a call to awakening. A call to rise above your limitations, to embrace the power that lies dormant within, and to walk in the fullness of your God-given destiny. Let this be a symphony of strength, a chorus of courage, a harmonious crescendo of faith that echoes throughout the ages.

Recognizing the Enemys Tactics

The enemy, like a cunning serpent, slithers through the shadows of our lives, whispering lies and weaving webs of deception. His goal is to blind us to God's truth, to sow seeds of doubt, and to steal our joy, our peace, and our freedom. He uses a variety of tactics, but some of the most common ones he employs are fear, doubt, and manipulation.

Fear is a powerful weapon that the enemy uses to paralyze us. He knows that if he can make us afraid, we will be less likely to step out in faith and pursue our dreams. He whispers in our ears, "What if you fail?" or "What if you get hurt?" He tries to convince us that we are not capable of handling the challenges that lie ahead. But the truth is, God has already given us everything we need to overcome fear. We can access his peace and courage through prayer and trust in his promises.

Doubt is another tool that the enemy uses to undermine our faith. He whispers, "You're not good enough," or "God doesn't really love you." He tries to convince us that we are unworthy of God's grace and love. But we need to remember that we are perfectly loved by God. He doesn't see our imperfections, but instead sees us as his masterpiece. He embraces us with love, forgiveness, and acceptance.

Manipulation is another tactic that the enemy uses to control us. He often uses other people to do his dirty work, subtly influencing us to make decisions that are not aligned with God's will. He might try to make us feel guilty for saying no or for standing up for what we believe in. But we must learn to discern the enemy's voice and to recognize his attempts to manipulate us. We must be vigilant and discern what is from

God and what is not. We must be discerning, knowing that he can use our emotions, our friends, our family members, our circumstances, and our fears to control us.

But God has given his daughters a power to fight back against the enemy: **discernment** . Discernment is the ability to see beyond the veil and recognize the enemy's tactics for what they are. It is the ability to perceive God's truth and to know His will for our lives.

Discernment is not a gift that is reserved for a select few; it is available to every believer. It is a skill that we can develop through prayer, Bible study, and practice. It is through these avenues that we can train ourselves to hear God's voice and to recognize the enemy's tactics.

As we learn to discern the enemy's tactics, we will be able to resist his temptations and walk in freedom. We will no longer be controlled by fear, doubt, and manipulation. We will be free to live out our God-given destiny and to fulfill the plans that God has for us.

Think of it this way: The enemy is like a con artist who is trying to sell you a fake product. He tries to convince you that his product is real and valuable, but in reality, it is worthless. But if you are discerning, you will be able to see through his lies and recognize the fake for what it is.

Discernment is essential for every woman of faith. It is the key to unlocking our true potential and living out our destiny in God.

When you're feeling afraid, stop and ask yourself, "Is this fear from God or from the enemy?" When you're feeling doubtful, stop and ask yourself, "Is this doubt from God or from the enemy?" And when you're being manipulated, stop

Seeing Beyond the Veil

The ability to discern truth from deception is a vital gift that allows women to see beyond the veil of illusion and perceive God's truth. It's like having spiritual x-ray vision, enabling you to penetrate the facades and understand the hidden agendas that can manipulate and hinder you. Imagine a world where you can navigate through the tangled paths of life with clarity, knowing the true intentions of those around you and the underlying motivations behind their actions. This is the power of discernment—a divine gift that allows you to see beyond the surface and understand the unseen forces at play.

Developing spiritual discernment is not an overnight process. It requires a conscious effort to cultivate a deep relationship with God, allowing Him to open your eyes to His truths. It's about training your spiritual senses, learning to recognize His voice and understand His language. It's about being sensitive to the subtle promptings of the Holy Spirit, allowing them to guide your decisions and shape your perceptions.

The enemy, however, is a master of deception, constantly seeking to cloud our minds and distort our perceptions. He throws out distractions, whispers lies, and fuels fears to keep us trapped in a cycle of confusion and doubt. He wants to blind us to the truth, keeping us from recognizing our true potential and fulfilling our God-given destiny. But the Lord, our loving Father, gives us the power to overcome these deceptions. He equips us with the tools and resources necessary to discern truth from falsehood.

Benefits of discernment

Discernment brings many benefits to our lives. Here are a few of them:

Increased freedom: Discernment helps us to break free from the enemy's control.
Greater peace: Discernment helps us to know God's will for our lives, which brings us peace.
Improved decision-making: Discernment helps us to make wise decisions that are aligned with God's will.
Stronger faith: Discernment helps us to grow in our faith and to become more like Jesus.

The enemy may be cunning, but God is stronger. By developing discernment, we can overcome the enemy's tactics, live in freedom, and fulfill our destiny in God.

better we will understand God's character and His ways.
3. **Seek wise counsel.** Talk to people who have a strong relationship with God and who can provide you with guidance. A trusted friend or pastor can help you discern God's voice.
4. **Be aware of your emotions.** The enemy often uses our emotions to manipulate us. If we are feeling afraid, anxious, or depressed, it is important to stop and ask ourselves if these emotions are from God or from the enemy.
5. **Pay attention to your thoughts.** Our thoughts can also be influenced by the enemy. If we are having negative or discouraging thoughts, it is important to challenge them and replace them with God's word.
6. **Trust your gut.** God often speaks to us through our intuition. If we have a strong feeling that something is not right, it is important to pay attention.

Steps to resisting the enemy's tactics

Recognize the enemy's voice: When the enemy is whispering lies in your ear, you need to recognize his voice. He often uses fear, doubt, and manipulation to control you. So when you are feeling these things, stop and ask yourself, "Is this from God or from the enemy?"
Seek truth: When the enemy is trying to deceive you, you need to seek the truth. The Bible is the ultimate source of truth. Read it, study it, and meditate on it.
Stand firm in your faith: When the enemy is trying to undermine your faith, you need to stand firm. Remember that you are loved and accepted by God. No matter what the enemy whispers to you, God is always with you.
Submit to God: When the enemy is trying to manipulate you, you need to submit to God. Give your life to Him and allow Him to lead you.
Pray for discernment: Ask God to give you wisdom and discernment. He will guide you if you ask Him to.

and ask yourself, "Is this manipulation from God or from the enemy?"

By asking these questions, we can begin to discern the enemy's tactics and resist his influence.

Discernment is not just about recognizing the enemy's tactics; it is also about understanding his motivations. The enemy's primary motivation is to steal, kill, and destroy (John 10:10). He wants to steal our joy, kill our dreams, and destroy our relationships. He wants to keep us from experiencing the fullness of God's love and blessings.

But God's motivation is to give us life to the full (John 10:10). He wants us to live in freedom, joy, and peace. He wants us to experience the fullness of His love and blessings.

By understanding the enemy's motivation, we can better resist his tactics. We can recognize his lies for what they are and stand firm in our faith.

Discernment is a powerful tool that can help us navigate the challenges of life and walk in victory. By developing this skill, we can overcome the enemy's tactics, live in freedom, and fulfill our destiny in God.

How to cultivate discernment

There are many ways to cultivate discernment. Here are a few tips:

1. **Spend time in prayer.** Prayer is the key to knowing God's will. Through prayer, we can open our hearts and minds to receive His guidance.
2. **Study the Bible.** The Bible is God's word and it is full of wisdom and guidance. The more we study the Bible, the

Imagine a woman walking through a marketplace, surrounded by vibrant colors, tempting scents, and enticing offers. She can easily get caught up in the allure of the moment, lured by superficial attractions and promises. But if she possesses spiritual discernment, she can see beyond the surface. She can recognize the deceptive practices, identify the true value of goods, and avoid getting ensnared by empty promises.

Discernment allows you to see beyond the facade of relationships, recognizing the true intentions of those around you. It helps you to discern between genuine love and manipulative tactics. It gives you the ability to understand the underlying motivations behind people's actions, leading to wise decisions and healthier relationships.

As you cultivate spiritual discernment, you will find yourself becoming more discerning in all areas of your life. You will be able to make wise choices regarding your finances, your career, and even your health. You will develop a heightened awareness of the spiritual realm, recognizing the presence of God's love and the enemy's attempts to deceive.

How do you develop this vital gift? It's a journey of faith and practice. Here are some practical steps you can take:

1. Seek God in the Secret Place:

Spend time in solitude, allowing God to speak to your heart. Listen to His still, small voice. Seek His guidance in your decisions and trust His wisdom to lead you. The more time you spend in His presence, the more sensitive you will become to His voice and promptings.

2. Immerse Yourself in God's Word:

Read the Bible regularly, meditating on its truths and allowing its words to penetrate your heart. Scripture is the foundation of discernment, providing a framework for understanding God's character, His will, and His plan for your life. It's like a spiritual map that guides you through the complexities of life, helping you navigate the twists and turns of the road.

3. Pray for Discernment:

Ask God to grant you the gift of discernment, to open your eyes to His truths and guide you through the maze of life. As you pray, be specific about your needs and ask for wisdom to see beyond the facades and understand the hidden agendas that can manipulate and hinder you.

4. Recognize Your Emotions:

Emotions are powerful indicators of spiritual truth. When you feel an uneasy feeling about a situation, person, or decision, it's often a sign from the Holy Spirit to take a step back and examine the situation more closely. Your intuition, guided by God's Spirit, can be a valuable tool in discerning truth.

5. Surround Yourself with Wise Counsel:

Seek the advice of spiritually mature mentors, trusted friends, and spiritual leaders who can provide you with wisdom and guidance. Discuss your concerns and challenges with them, seeking their insights and perspectives on the matters you're struggling with.

6. Practice Faithfulness:

As you cultivate spiritual discernment, you will experience times of doubt, confusion, and uncertainty. But don't let these challenges discourage you. Stay faithful to God, trusting His guidance and His promises. Continue to seek His wisdom and allow Him to shape your perceptions.

Cultivating spiritual discernment is a lifelong journey. It's a process of growing in faith, seeking God's guidance, and developing your spiritual senses. As you embrace this gift, you will find yourself navigating the complexities of life with clarity, making wise choices, and living in alignment with God's will. You will experience a new level of freedom, peace, and joy as you walk in the light of His truth.

Imagine the impact that spiritual discernment can have on your life and your relationships. Picture yourself moving through the world with clarity, knowing the true intentions of those around you and making wise choices that align with God's will. This is the power of discerning truth—a gift that empowers you to see beyond the veil of deception and embrace a life filled with purpose, meaning, and divine guidance.

Understanding Divine Communication

The language of the Spirit is a symphony of whispers, visions, and inner promptings, a tapestry woven with divine threads that guide us through the complexities of life. It is a communication that transcends the limits of our human understanding, a bridge between the finite and the infinite, a communion with the very heart of God.

Imagine a world where you could hear the whispers of heaven, where you could see glimpses of the unseen realm, where you could feel the gentle nudges of divine guidance. This is the world of spiritual discernment, the realm where we learn to listen with our hearts, see with our souls, and understand the language of the Spirit.

The Spirit speaks to us in myriad ways, each unique and tailored to our individual needs and receptivity. Sometimes, it speaks through the gentle rustling of leaves, a poignant melody, or a chance encounter that holds a deeper meaning. Other times, it speaks through vivid dreams, breathtaking visions, or the quiet, compelling voice of our intuition.

Dreams, those nocturnal journeys into the realm of the subconscious, often serve as a conduit for divine communication. They can be prophetic, revealing future events or unveiling hidden truths about our lives. They can be symbolic, using imagery to communicate spiritual principles or guide us towards a specific path. They can be transformative, bringing about a shift in our consciousness or revealing a new understanding of ourselves and our purpose.

Visions, those flashes of insight that illuminate our minds, are another powerful means of divine communication. They can be fleeting glimpses of the unseen realm, profound revelations that change our perspectives, or powerful promptings that guide our actions. They can be visual, auditory, or even tactile, each modality conveying a unique message from the Spirit.

Inner promptings, those quiet intuitions that arise within us, are a subtle but profound form of divine guidance. They can be a gentle nudge in the right direction, a warning against a potential danger, or a deep knowing that aligns us with God's will. These promptings often come in the form of a strong feeling, an intuitive knowing, or a sudden conviction that something is right or wrong.

To understand the language of the Spirit, we must first cultivate a deep and intimate relationship with God. This involves spending time in prayer, meditating on his Word, and seeking his presence in all areas of our lives. We must also develop a willingness to listen, to be receptive to his voice, and to trust in his guidance.

As we journey through life, we will inevitably encounter crossroads and challenges. It is in these moments that the language of the Spirit becomes crucial. We need to discern his voice amidst the noise of the world, to trust his guidance, and to make decisions that are aligned with his will.

Here are some practical ways to cultivate spiritual discernment:

Seek God's presence regularly: Spend time in prayer, meditation, and Bible study, creating a space for communion with God.
Cultivate a listening heart: Develop a habit of listening attentively to the whispers of the Spirit, both within and around you.

Pay attention to dreams and visions: Keep a dream journal and record any vivid or significant dreams. Pay attention to any recurring themes or symbols. If you experience visions, note the details and seek God's interpretation.

Trust your intuition: Your intuition is a powerful tool for discernment. Learn to recognize and trust the inner promptings that arise within you.

Seek guidance from spiritual mentors: Find wise and discerning individuals who can offer guidance and support in your spiritual journey.

Ask for God's discernment: Pray specifically for God to grant you discernment, to open your eyes to his truth, and to lead you in the right direction.

Spiritual discernment is a gift, a treasure to be cultivated and nurtured. It is a powerful tool that can empower us to navigate the complexities of life with confidence, to make wise decisions, and to live a life that is aligned with God's will.

As we learn to hear the language of the Spirit, we open ourselves to a world of possibilities, a world where we can experience God's presence and power in every aspect of our lives. This is a journey that requires humility, a willingness to learn, and a deep desire to know God more fully. It is a journey that will transform our lives and lead us to a greater understanding of our true identity and purpose.

Beyond the realm of dreams, visions, and inner promptings, there are other ways the Spirit communicates. He may use the words of others to speak to you, a song that captures your heart, or a natural phenomenon that speaks to your soul.

Sometimes, the Spirit reveals truths through unexpected circumstances or challenges. These experiences, while often uncomfortable, can be profound learning opportunities, shaping our character and deepening our faith.

It is essential to remember that the Spirit speaks in a way that is unique to each individual. There is no one-size-fits-all approach to hearing his voice.

The key is to be receptive, to cultivate a listening heart, and to trust in his guidance. The more we practice spiritual discernment, the more attuned we become to his voice.

Just as a musician learns to discern the nuances of different instruments in an orchestra, we learn to discern the different ways the Spirit speaks to us. We learn to recognize his voice amidst the noise of the world, to decipher his messages, and to respond with obedience and faith.

Spiritual discernment is an ongoing journey. It is a process of growth, a deepening of our relationship with God, and an increasing awareness of his presence and guidance in our lives. It is a gift that empowers us to live with purpose, to make wise decisions, and to experience the fullness of God's grace.

Remember, the Spirit is always with us, always speaking, always guiding us towards our destiny. It is up to us to cultivate our spiritual ears and eyes, to open our hearts and minds, and to embrace the language of the Spirit.

And in doing so, we will discover a world of possibilities, a world where we can truly walk in the light of God's truth, where we can hear his voice clearly, and where we can live out our destinies with confidence and joy.

Making Wise Decisions with Gods Guidance

Imagine standing at a crossroads, each path leading to a different destination. You feel the weight of the decision before you, the unknown stretching out ahead. You long for clarity, for a guiding hand to lead you to the right path. This is where discernment comes in, the ability to hear God's voice amidst the noise of life, to see beyond the distractions and align your choices with His will.

Discernment isn't just about picking the "right" option; it's about aligning your will with God's, allowing His wisdom to shape your decisions and lead you to His intended path. It's about recognizing the subtle whispers of the Holy Spirit, the inner promptings that guide you towards His purpose.

The world around us is filled with competing voices, each vying for our attention. We're bombarded with messages through social media, news, and even those closest to us, each pushing us towards a different direction. How do we navigate this cacophony of voices and discern the true path God has laid out for us?

The first step is to recognize the enemy's tactics. He is a master of disguise, often appearing as a friend offering seemingly harmless advice, a gentle voice whispering doubts and fears, a subtle temptation that promises temporary fulfillment. He uses fear, manipulation, and self-doubt to distract us from God's plan, to lead us astray from the path of righteousness.

But God has equipped us with the tools to see beyond the veil of deception. He has given us the gift of spiritual vision, the ability to perceive His truth and discern His voice. Think of it as a spiritual compass, guiding us towards His intended direction, even when the path seems unclear.

This spiritual vision is cultivated through a deep connection with God. It's found in the quiet moments of prayer, meditation, and Bible study, where we can truly tune into His voice. The more we spend time in His presence, the more attuned we become to His promptings, His subtle whispers of direction.

God speaks to us in various ways: through dreams, visions, and inner promptings. He might use a verse in Scripture, a song on the radio, or even a conversation with a friend to communicate His will. It's important to learn to recognize His voice, to become sensitive to those subtle nudges that lead us towards His purpose.

Discernment is also about taking the time to seek God's guidance in every decision. When faced with a choice, take the time to reflect, to pray, and to listen. Ask God for wisdom and clarity, and be willing to wait on His answer.

Here are some practical tools and strategies to aid your discernment journey:

Embrace silence and solitude: Schedule time for quiet reflection, where you can shut out the noise of the world and listen for God's voice.
Engage in spiritual practices: Cultivate a deeper connection with God through prayer, meditation, and Scripture study.
Seek guidance from trusted spiritual mentors: Connect with mature believers who can offer wisdom and insight into your specific situation.
Pay attention to your inner promptings: Become attuned to the subtle nudges of the Holy Spirit, the inner whispers

that guide you towards God's will.
Keep a prayer journal: Write down your prayers, your thoughts, and any insights you receive. This will help you track God's guidance over time.
Trust your intuition: When making a decision, allow your intuition to guide you. This is the inner voice of wisdom that God has placed within you.

Remember, discernment isn't a one-time event; it's an ongoing process of seeking God's will, trusting His guidance, and aligning your choices with His purpose. It's about surrendering your plans to His, allowing Him to lead you to the path He has designed for you.

As you journey deeper into God's will, you'll experience a growing confidence in His guidance. You'll begin to recognize His voice more clearly, and you'll develop a greater trust in His plan for your life.

Remember, God is always with you, guiding you, empowering you, and leading you to the fulfillment of your destiny.

Unveiling Gods Truth through Scripture

The Word of God is a powerful instrument, a living force that can transform lives and reshape destinies. It's not just a collection of ancient stories or a set of rules to follow. It's a map, a compass, and a guide to lead us into the fullness of our God-given potential. Every word breathed out by the Creator carries the potential to unlock a hidden door, unveil a hidden truth, and ignite a fire in our hearts that burns with divine purpose.

Imagine a seed tucked away in the earth, waiting for the right moment to sprout. It may seem dormant, but life is pulsating within it. The same is true for the Word of God. It may seem like simple words on a page, but within those words lies the power to break chains, heal wounds, and awaken dormant dreams. The Word is the seed of our destiny, waiting to be planted in the fertile soil of our hearts. It's a promise whispered on the wind, a beacon of hope shining in the darkest night.

As we open our hearts to the Word, allowing it to penetrate our innermost being, something extraordinary begins to happen. It's like a gentle but powerful current, moving us towards the destiny that God has already ordained for us. The Word becomes a sword that cuts through the lies we've believed, a shield that protects us from the arrows of doubt and fear. It's a wellspring of wisdom that guides our every step and a source of strength that empowers us to overcome any obstacle.

But the Word is not meant to be a passive observer in our lives. It's meant to be engaged, embraced, and experienced. We must spend time in God's presence, immersing ourselves respond to His promptings, and allow His words to shape your thoughts, your emotions, and your actions.

These are just a few of the many ways to cultivate intimacy with God. It's a journey, not a destination, and it takes time, dedication, and a willingness to be vulnerable. But the rewards are immeasurable.

As you spend time with God in the secret place, you'll experience His love, His peace, His guidance, and His power in ways you never imagined. You'll discover the true meaning of your life, the purpose for which you were created, and the boundless potential that lies within you.

In the secret place, you'll be empowered to live a life of purpose, a life of joy, a life that makes a difference in the world. You'll find your voice, your strength, your freedom, and your destiny, all through a deeper connection with the one who created you.

Claiming Your Power in Christ

The enemy knows that when a woman steps into her authority, it shakes the very foundations of his kingdom. He knows that her power in Christ is a force to be reckoned with, a force that can change the world, a force that can bring healing and restoration, a force that can shatter his strongholds and dismantle his schemes.

So he tries to keep her bound, to hold her captive in fear and doubt. He whispers lies in her ear, telling her that she's not enough, that she's not worthy, that she's not capable. He tries to convince her that she's better off playing small, better off staying silent, better off letting him control her destiny.

But the Lord has a different plan. He's not interested in silencing women; He's interested in setting them free. He's not interested in limiting their potential; He's interested in seeing them rise to their full glory. He's not interested in their staying small; He's interested in seeing them become giants in faith, giants in power, giants in love.

And the authority that He's given them is not something to be feared or shied away from. It's a gift, a privilege, a power that can transform not only their own lives but the lives of those around them. It's a power that can heal the sick, deliver the captive, and bring hope to the hopeless.

So how do you, as women, step into this authority that Christ has given you? How do you claim our power and begin to wield it for good?

It starts with an understanding. You must understand that you are not powerless. you are not insignificant. You are not meant to be passive observers in this world; you are meant to be active participants, shaping the world around you with the power of God working through you.

You are the daughters of the King, and He has given you a kingdom to rule (Zion). This is not just a spiritual kingdom, but it also reflects on how we see and impact the world around you. His authority is ours, and our authority is His.

But this authority is not given to you as a weapon to wield against others, but as a force for good, a force for healing, a force for transformation.

You are to use this power to love, to serve, to heal, to restore, to build up, to inspire, to empower, to encourage, to make a difference in the world for good.

It starts with understanding the power you have been given.

But understanding is only the beginning. You must also learn to wield this power effectively.

Here are some practical ways you can start to step into our authority and claim our power in Christ:

Speak up with boldness. Don't be afraid to share your voice. Don't be afraid to speak truth. Don't be afraid to stand up for what you believe in. The world needs to hear your voice. Your voice is powerful, and it can change the world. The Lord desires you to speak truth to power, but He desires you to also speak to people with grace and love. Your words can be a powerful weapon for the kingdom of God, but also can be a source of encouragement and hope to others.
Live with intention. Don't live your life by chance. Don't let the enemy dictate your path. Be intentional in everything you do. Live with a purpose, with a goal, with a mission.

Ask the Lord what He desires for you to do, what He wants to see you accomplish, and live in alignment with His will. Let your life be a testament to the power of God.
Embrace your gifts. God has given each of us unique gifts and talents. Don't be afraid to use them. Don't be afraid to shine. Don't be afraid to be you. Your gifts are a blessing to the world, and they can make a real difference.

Remember, you are not defined by your circumstances, your past, or your failures. You are defined by the Word of God, and by His love.

Seek His wisdom. Don't rely on your own understanding. Don't try to figure it all out on your own. Ask God for wisdom. Seek His guidance in every decision. Trust His plans for you, even when you don't understand them.
Be a woman of prayer. Prayer is a powerful weapon, and it's one of the most important ways to step into our authority. When we pray, we connect with the power of God, and we give Him the opportunity to work through us. Make prayer a priority in your life.

Here are some additional tips to remember:

Don't be afraid to fail. Failure is a part of life. It's how we learn and grow. But don't let failure define you. Get up, dust yourself off, and keep moving forward.
Don't let the enemy steal your joy. The enemy wants to see you defeated and discouraged. Don't let him win. Find joy in Christ. Find joy in your purpose. Find joy in serving others.
Surrender your will to His. The most powerful thing you can do is surrender your will to the Lord. Let Him lead you. Let Him guide you. Trust His plan, even when it's hard.
Don't compare yourself to others. We are all unique creations of God, and we are all called to different things.

Don't compare yourself to others and try to be like them. Be you. Embrace your uniqueness.

The authority that Christ has given us is a powerful gift. It's a gift that can change the world. It's a gift that can bring healing, restoration, and hope. It's a gift that can set us free.

But it's up to us to claim it. It's up to us to embrace it. It's up to us to wield it for good.

Step into your authority. Claim you power in Christ. Make a difference in the world.

You are daughters of the King, and you have a real kingdom to rule not just in the spiritual.

Let us not underestimate the power that you have been given. You can change the world through your faith and love.

The enemy has a plan to try and hold women back, but the Lord has a plan to set you free.

It is time for you to rise to your full potential, to claim your power, and to fulfill your destiny image.

in His Word. Read it, study it, meditate on it, let it fill your mind and your heart. The more we allow ourselves to be transformed by the Word, the more we will see the world through God's eyes, and the more our lives will align with His perfect plan.

This is the power of the Word: it's not just information; it's life itself. It's a living, breathing entity that interacts with us, molds us, and changes us from the inside out. As we open our hearts to the Word, we open ourselves to a world of endless possibilities. We unlock a door to a destiny beyond our wildest dreams.

The Word of God is like a lamp, shining brightly in the darkness, illuminating the path ahead. It's like a powerful magnet, pulling us towards the fullness of God's purpose for our lives. It's like a powerful key, unlocking doors to a future we could never have imagined.

Some might say, "I've heard it all before. I know the Bible stories." But there's a difference between simply knowing the words and truly allowing the Word to penetrate your being. It's not just about memorizing verses or reciting doctrines; it's about letting the Word shape your thoughts, your actions, and your entire perspective.

Take, for example, the story of Ruth, a young woman who found herself in a foreign land, facing an uncertain future. But she clung to the promise of God's faithfulness, and as a result, her life was transformed. She became an ancestor of Jesus Christ, her story woven into the very fabric of God's redemptive plan. Her faithfulness to God, her willingness to trust His plan, and her unwavering dedication to His Word ultimately led to an outcome far greater than anything she could have imagined.

Or consider the story of Esther, a young woman who was chosen by God to be queen, not for her own glory, but to save her people from annihilation. Esther's life was a tapestry of faith, courage, and obedience to God's will. She was willing to risk everything, to stand against the tide of opposition, to fight for what was right, all because she knew that God had a plan for her. She listened to the whispers of God's voice, she trusted in His strength, and she stepped into the destiny He had prepared for her. And in doing so, she became a symbol of hope and resilience, a testament to the power of God's Word to transform lives.

There are countless stories throughout scripture, stories that illustrate the power of the Word to transform lives, to empower women, and to set them on a path towards their destiny. These stories aren't just ancient tales; they are living testimonies, reminders of the power that lies within God's Word. They are echoes of His faithfulness, His love, and His unwavering commitment to those who seek Him with a sincere heart.

The power of the Word lies not just in the words themselves, but in the One who breathed them into existence. It's the Word of God that carries the weight of His authority, the power of His presence, and the promise of His love. It's through His Word that we connect with His heart, His mind, and His eternal plan. It's the Word that guides our steps, empowers our choices, and leads us to a life of purpose and significance.

Don't underestimate the power of the Word. It's not just a book; it's a force, a light, and a life-changing reality. It has the power to transform your life, to reshape your destiny, and to set you on a path towards the greatness that God has already ordained for you.

As you open the pages of God's Word, open your heart as well. Allow yourself to be transformed by its power. Allow it to penetrate your soul, to awaken your spirit, and to guide you towards the destiny that God has planned for you. And as you do, you'll begin to experience the fullness of His love, the power of His presence, and the promise of a life lived to the fullest. For it's through His Word that we connect with His heart, His mind, and His eternal plan. It's the Word that guides our steps, empowers our choices, and leads us to a life of purpose and significance.

The Word of God is a treasure, a gift, and a key to unlocking the destiny God has placed within you. Embrace it, cherish it, and let it transform your life. For within its pages lies the power to set you free, to guide you towards your destiny, and to lead you into a life that overflows with the love and grace of the Almighty.

Unveiling the Unseen Realm

Imagine a vast tapestry, woven with threads of gold and silver, each representing a whispered prayer rising to the heavens. This tapestry is a breathtaking mosaic of our hopes, dreams, and deepest desires, and it is in this tapestry that we find the power of prayer—an unseen realm of connection that shapes our lives and alters our destinies.

Prayer isn't a mere ritual; it's a sacred dance between our souls and the Divine. It's the opening of our hearts to a love that transcends understanding, a love that transforms not only our inner world but also our external circumstances. When we pray, we're not simply making requests; we're engaging in a conversation, a communion with the very source of all power.

Picture a child reaching out for their parent's hand, seeking guidance and comfort. That's the essence of prayer—a childlike trust in the wisdom and love of our Heavenly Father. He is not a distant, unapproachable God, but a loving Father who yearns to hear our voice, to know our heart, and to guide our steps.

Prayer is a conduit, a channel through which God pours His grace and strength into our lives. It's the key that unlocks hidden reservoirs of power within us, enabling us to overcome obstacles, break free from limitations, and walk in the fullness of our God-given potential.

Consider the story of Elijah, the prophet who stood alone against the prophets of Baal on Mount Carmel. Faced with overwhelming odds, he prayed with unwavering faith. His prayer wasn't a desperate plea, but a bold declaration of

God's power. And the Lord answered, sending fire from heaven to consume the sacrifice, proving His authority and demonstrating Elijah's faith.

This is the power of prayer—it shifts the atmosphere, ignites divine intervention, and sets in motion the very will of God. It isn't about our words, but about our hearts—our surrender to the divine, our trust in His sovereignty, and our unwavering belief in His promises.

The tapestry of prayer is a testament to the transformative power of connection. It's a reminder that we are not alone in our struggles, that we are held in the loving embrace of our Creator, and that our prayers, woven into the fabric of His will, have the power to change not only our lives but the course of history.

The tapestry of prayer is a powerful reminder that God is not bound by time or space, that His presence is ever-present, and that our prayers, woven into the fabric of His will, have the power to change not only our lives but the course of history.

Imagine a tapestry, not merely woven with threads of gold and silver, but with threads of every color imaginable. Each color representing a unique individual, each thread a prayer, and each prayer echoing the heart's desire. This tapestry is a testament to the diversity of God's people and the power of prayer to unite us, to break down barriers, and to create a beautiful and harmonious symphony of faith.

Prayer is a bridge that connects us to one another, transcending differences and uniting us in a common pursuit of the divine. We pray for our loved ones, for our communities, and for the world, weaving threads of love and compassion into the tapestry of humanity.

In the tapestry of prayer, we find solace in our grief, strength in our weakness, and hope in our despair. We find a refuge from the storms of life, a place where our burdens are lifted and our hearts are renewed. And we find the courage to step forward, not in our own strength, but in the strength of the One who hears our every plea.

Prayer isn't simply a means to obtain things; it's a means to grow closer to the heart of God. It's a journey of discovery, a quest to know Him more deeply, to understand His love, and to become more like Him.

As we pray, we are transformed. Our perspectives shift, our priorities align, and our hearts are molded into His image. We become more compassionate, more forgiving, more loving, and more like the God we seek.

The tapestry of prayer is an invitation, a call to step into the unseen realm, a realm where our faith takes flight and our destinies are shaped by the divine. It's an invitation to experience the power of prayer, not just in our personal lives, but in the lives of those around us, creating ripples of hope and transformation that extend far beyond ourselves.

So, embrace the power of prayer. Seek Him in the secret place, where your heart can freely speak and your spirit can soar. Let your prayers rise like incense, filling the air with the fragrance of your devotion. And watch as God's hand weaves your life into the beautiful tapestry of His will.

Let your prayers be a symphony of faith, a chorus of hope, and a testament to the transformative power of connection. Let your prayers be a beacon of light, illuminating the path for others, and let them be a testament to the love and grace of the One who hears every whispered plea.

Trusting Gods Promises

Walking by faith is not always easy. It's like stepping into a dark room, trusting that there is a light switch somewhere, even though you can't see it. There are moments when doubt creeps in, whispering, "What if there's no light? What if you stumble and fall?" But faith isn't about blind certainty; it's about trusting a promise, even when you can't see the evidence. It's about clinging to hope, even when circumstances seem hopeless.

Imagine a young woman named Sarah. She dreamed of becoming a doctor, but her family was struggling financially. She felt the weight of their expectations, knowing that they wouldn't be able to afford her education. She started to doubt her dream, telling herself it was just a fantasy, an impossible goal.

Then, one evening, she was reading the Bible and stumbled upon a verse: "For I know the plans I have for you," declares the Lord, "plans to prosper you and not to harm you, plans to give you hope and a future." (Jeremiah 29:11).

Sarah's heart stirred. She remembered her dream, the one she'd almost abandoned. Could this verse be a message from God, a promise that He had a plan for her?

She decided to pray, asking God to guide her, to show her a path toward her dream. She continued to study hard, praying for opportunities and financial support. And, against all odds, doors started to open. She received scholarships, unexpected donations, and a kind mentor who helped her navigate the challenges of medical school.

Sarah's journey was not without its struggles. There were times when she doubted, when fear threatened to overwhelm her. But she clung to the promise she'd found in Jeremiah 29:11. She trusted that God was with her, leading her every step of the way.

Sarah graduated medical school and became a doctor, fulfilling her dream. It wasn't an easy path, but she learned that faith is not just about believing in something; it's about trusting in the One who promises to guide you, to sustain you, and to see you through.

The Bible is filled with stories of people who walked by faith. Abraham, for example, left his home and family, trusting in God's promise to give him a new land. He faced many challenges, but he never lost sight of God's faithfulness.

And then there's David, a young shepherd boy who trusted in God's promise to give him victory over the giant Goliath. He faced an opponent who seemed invincible, yet he believed in God's strength and power. He went out with courage and faith, and God gave him the victory.

These stories, and countless others, remind us that faith is not about being blind to the world; it's about seeing beyond the limitations of our own eyes and trusting in the promises of God. It's about believing in the invisible, knowing that there is a God who loves us, who cares for us, and who has a plan for our lives.

But faith is not a passive thing. It's a living, active force. It's not enough to just believe in God; we must trust in Him. We must surrender our will to His, allowing Him to guide and lead us. We must take steps of obedience, even when we don't fully understand.

When we walk by faith, we are not just trusting in God's promises for our lives, but we are also releasing control and allowing Him to work in and through us. It's a beautiful, liberating experience, even though it can be challenging at times.

The world tells us to focus on the tangible, on what we can see and touch. It tells us to be practical, to be realistic, to not get our hopes up. But God's Word tells us something different. It tells us to walk by faith, not by sight. It tells us to believe in the impossible, to trust in the unseen.

As we journey through life, there will be times when we face uncertainty, when we feel lost and alone. But these are the moments when our faith is tested, when we have the opportunity to choose to trust in God. We can choose to see the world through His eyes, to believe in His promises, and to walk forward with faith and hope.

The path of faith is not always easy, but it's always worth it. For when we choose to trust in God, we open ourselves to a life filled with purpose, meaning, and abundance beyond our wildest dreams. We discover that God's promises are not just words on a page; they are living realities that can transform our lives and empower us to live out our destinies.

Releasing Control and Trusting Gods Will

The whisper of surrender is a gentle breeze that carries us into the depths of God's embrace, a place where our own will melts away and His perfect plan takes shape. It's not about giving up on our dreams or abandoning our passions, but rather about letting go of the need to control every detail of our lives. It's about recognizing that our human understanding is limited and that God's wisdom far surpasses our own.

Imagine a sculptor meticulously crafting a magnificent masterpiece. The clay, initially formless, is molded and shaped with precision, each stroke revealing a hidden beauty. We, too, are in the hands of a divine artist, and surrendering to His will is like allowing Him to shape us into the most exquisite versions of ourselves.

This surrender is not a passive resignation but an active choice, a decision to trust in God's unwavering love and faithfulness. It's about recognizing that He has a grand plan for our lives, a plan that transcends our limited perspectives and leads us to a future far brighter than we could ever imagine.

The journey of surrender may not always be easy. There will be moments when our human desires clash with God's will, times when we feel tempted to regain control or question His motives. But it's precisely in these moments of uncertainty that we must cling to His promises, reminding ourselves that He is good, He is faithful, and His plans are always for our ultimate benefit.

Let's look to the example of Hannah, a woman who yearned for a child but faced barrenness. Desperate for a child, she poured out her heart to God in the temple, vowing to dedicate her child to His service. Her surrender, a heartfelt act of trust, moved God's heart, and in His time, she was blessed with a son, Samuel, who went on to become a mighty prophet.

Hannah's story reminds us that surrender is not a sign of weakness, but a testament to our faith. It's about letting go of our own agenda and embracing God's will for our lives. It's about trusting that He knows what's best, even when we can't see the bigger picture.

Surrender is not a one-time event but an ongoing process. It's a daily choice to seek His guidance, to listen to His voice, and to trust in His perfect timing. It's about letting go of the need to control, to micromanage our lives, and instead, embrace the freedom that comes with living in complete dependence on God.

In the secret place, where we connect with God on a deeper level, our hearts become more receptive to His whispers. We begin to see life through His eyes, recognizing the beauty in the midst of challenges and the purpose in every circumstance. Surrender becomes a dance, a beautiful choreography of faith, where our will aligns with His, creating a symphony of joy and fulfillment.

As we step into this dance of surrender, we experience a profound freedom. We are released from the burden of control, the anxiety of making our own way, and the fear of the unknown. We find peace in His presence, knowing that He holds us securely in His hands, guiding us toward our destiny.

This surrender is a journey of transformation, a process that molds us into the image of Christ, shaping us into vessels of His love, grace, and power. It's a journey that requires faith, courage, and a willingness to let go of our own plans and embrace His perfect will.

Think of it as climbing a mountain. We can try to climb it on our own, straining and struggling with every step, or we can choose to trust a skilled guide, who knows the best path, the safest routes, and the most breathtaking views. Surrendering to God is like choosing that guide, allowing Him to lead us through the challenges and triumphs, ultimately leading us to the summit of His purpose.

So, dear sisters, let's embrace the art of surrender. Step into the secret place, where your hearts meet His, and allow Him to guide you through the tapestry of your destinies. In the surrender, you will find true freedom, lasting joy, and a life that reflects His glory.

Writing as a Tool for Revelation

In the quiet hush of a solitary room, with pen in hand and heart yearning for divine connection, a potent transformation takes place. It is within this sacred space, where words flow from the depths of our souls, that we encounter the very breath of God. Writing, often seen as a mere act of expression, becomes a conduit, a pathway to unlock the hidden depths of revelation, a portal to the prophetic voice that whispers within.

Imagine a room bathed in the soft glow of morning light, a steaming mug of coffee beside a notebook waiting patiently to be filled with the secrets of the heart. As the pen glides across the paper, a torrent of thoughts and emotions erupts. It's not just a personal journal, but a sacred chronicle, a tapestry woven with threads of divine insight and prophetic whispers. The mundane act of putting pen to paper morphs into a spiritual practice, a journey of discovery where the heart meets the mind and both find solace in the embrace of the Divine.

The written word is more than just ink on paper; it's a tangible manifestation of the unseen world. Each stroke, each sentence, carries the weight of a divine message, a testament to the presence of the Almighty in the everyday. It's like holding a shard of light, a fragment of God's truth, and allowing its radiance to illuminate the hidden corners of our hearts and minds.

Think of the prophets of old. Isaiah, Jeremiah, Ezekiel, and countless others – their words flowed from a heart ablaze with the fire of God's revelation. Their prophetic pronouncements were not mere pronouncements, but a symphony of truth, a tapestry woven with threads of divine inspiration. These were not mere men and women, but vessels, conduits through which God's voice resonated. The power of their words shaped nations, transformed lives, and echoed throughout history.

You, too, have the privilege of carrying this prophetic mantle, not as pronouncements of doom and gloom, but as messages of hope, encouragement, and love. Your words, penned with intention and fueled by the fire of the Spirit, can ignite the hearts of others, stir dormant desires, and ignite the spark of faith.

This is not about conjuring words out of thin air, but about aligning our hearts with God's will. The prophet's heart is a symphony of obedience, a tapestry woven with threads of surrender. It's about surrendering the pen to the hand of the Master Artist, allowing the ink to flow with the rhythm of the Divine.

The journey of unlocking the prophetic voice begins with a deep yearning for God, a thirst for His truth. It's about cultivating a listening heart, an open mind, and a soul that vibrates with the anticipation of God's revelation. This yearning is not a passive longing, but an active pursuit, a relentless search for the hidden treasures that lie buried deep within the scriptures, in the whispers of the Holy Spirit, and in the experiences that shape our lives.

The practice of writing as a tool for revelation is not about seeking prophetic pronouncements for the sake of sensationalism. It's about delving into the depths of our own souls, excavating the truths that lie hidden within. It's about allowing God's voice to resonate through us, not as a substitute for His word, but as a complement, a symphony

Imagine, years from now, revisiting your journal entries, reliving the triumphs, the challenges, and the miracles that God has orchestrated. It's a treasure trove of memories, a testament to the transformative power of His grace. You'll see how far you've come, how God has shaped you, and how He has faithfully guided your steps.

As you embark on this journey of journaling, let your pen become an instrument of faith, a conduit for revelation, and a tool for transforming your life. Write with intention, write with honesty, and write with expectation. Expect to hear from God, expect to see His hand at work in your life, and expect to experience the power of His presence.

Here are some practical tips to make journaling a regular part of your spiritual practice:

Find a quiet place: Set aside a time and space where you can be alone with God. This might be a cozy corner of your home, a peaceful park, or a quiet retreat.
Create a ritual: Develop a simple routine to help you transition into a state of prayer and contemplation. This might involve lighting a candle, listening to soothing music, or reading a scripture verse.
Be honest with yourself: Write with honesty and vulnerability. Don't be afraid to express your doubts, your fears, and your desires.
Expect God's presence: Believe that God is with you, that He wants to speak to you, and that He wants to guide you.
Don't be afraid to be creative: Use your journaling as a space to explore your creativity, to express your faith through poetry, prose, or even art.
Revisit your entries: Set aside time to read through your journal entries. Reflect on the insights you have gained, the lessons you have learned, and the progress you have made.

Remember, dear sisters, the power of the written word is a gift from God. It's a tool to unlock the depths of our souls, to release prophetic truth, and to record the journey of our faith. Embrace the power of journaling, and allow it to become a transformative force in your life.

Penning Gods Word for Transformation

The art of prophetic writing is a sacred dance, a delicate interplay between the human pen and the divine breath. It's not simply about putting words on paper; it's about allowing the very essence of God's heart to flow through you, shaping the words into a powerful conduit of revelation and transformation.

Think of yourself as a vessel, a channel for the divine symphony to resonate through your soul. As you surrender to the Holy Spirit's guidance, your pen becomes an instrument of truth, painting vivid portraits of God's will and purpose for the world. This art form is not just about writing words but about weaving a tapestry of God's truth, one thread of revelation at a time.

Writing prophetic messages is an act of obedience, a response to the divine call to speak truth into the darkness. It requires a heart attuned to God's voice, a mind open to His whispers, and a spirit willing to be molded into His image. It's a journey of intimacy with God, where your words become a reflection of His love, His wisdom, and His power.

To embark on this journey of prophetic writing, you must first cultivate a deep and abiding relationship with God. Spend time in the secret place, allowing His presence to envelop you, saturating your soul with His truth. Immerse yourself in His Word, allowing it to shape your thoughts and guide your heart.

Then, as you listen with attentive ears, you'll begin to discern the gentle whispers of the Holy Spirit. It might be a song in your heart, a vision in your mind, or a quiet prompting within your spirit. Pay attention to these promptings, for they are the raw materials of your prophetic writing.

As you write, remember that clarity is paramount. Your words should be a beacon of truth, illuminating the path for those who are lost or searching. God's message must be conveyed with precision and authenticity, ensuring that it resonates with the hearts and minds of those who read it.

Accuracy is also crucial. Let your words be anchored in Scripture, reflecting the truth of God's Word. Don't be afraid to consult the Bible, seeking guidance and confirmation from its timeless wisdom. The prophetic voice, while inspired by the Holy Spirit, must always align with the teachings of God's Word.

But remember, writing prophetically is more than just intellectual understanding; it's an act of faith, an outpouring of God's love. Your words should be infused with compassion, grace, and a deep sense of God's mercy. Let your pen be a tool of encouragement, offering hope to the weary and strength to the discouraged.

As you write, allow your heart to overflow with the love of God. Let your words be a fragrant offering, carrying the sweet aroma of His grace into the world. Each sentence should be a prayer, a whispered plea for God's blessings to be poured out upon those who read it.

The power of written revelation lies in its ability to transform lives. Your words can be a catalyst for healing, restoration, and spiritual growth. They can ignite faith, inspire hope, and propel others towards their God-given destiny.

But remember, you are not the source of the message. You are merely a conduit, a vessel through which God's truth flows. Humility is essential, acknowledging that the power behind the words rests in the divine hand of God.

So, as you embark on this journey of prophetic writing, remember that your words have the potential to change the world. Let your pen be a tool of transformation, bringing hope, healing, and revelation to a world that desperately needs it.

The prophetic voice is a powerful force, a whisper from heaven that can shake the foundations of the world. And in the hands of a humble and obedient writer, it can be a catalyst for change, a spark that ignites a fire of faith, hope, and love.

Let your writing be a testament to God's love, a beacon of hope, and a powerful message of truth that will resonate through generations to come.

Remember, your words have power. Let them be a testament to God's glory, a reflection of His love, and a beacon of hope for a world that needs His touch.

Leaving a Mark on the World

In the vast landscape of human experience, writing has always held a profound power. It has the ability to capture the essence of our thoughts, emotions, and experiences, shaping narratives that transcend time and connect with the hearts and minds of others. For women of faith, writing can be a particularly powerful tool, a conduit through which God's message flows, impacting the world in profound and lasting ways. It's not simply about putting words on paper, but about wielding the pen as a weapon of spiritual warfare, crafting stories that ignite hope, inspire faith, and leave a legacy of truth and inspiration.

Think of your writing as a testament to the divine work taking place within you. Each sentence, each paragraph, each story is a reflection of God's grace in your life, a testament to the transformative power of His love. As you delve into the depths of your soul, allowing God's Spirit to guide your hand, you will unveil hidden truths, tap into the wellspring of divine inspiration, and pen words that resonate with the deepest yearnings of the human spirit.

Imagine your writing as a bridge connecting generations, spanning the chasm of time to deliver God's message to those who need it most. Your words can illuminate the path for others, offering guidance, comfort, and strength in their own spiritual journeys. They can be a source of encouragement during times of doubt, a beacon of hope in the midst of darkness, a reminder of the enduring power of God's love.

Think of Esther, a young woman thrust into a position of power and responsibility. Her bravery and courage in confronting the evil Haman, her willingness to risk her life for her people, were not just a matter of circumstance. It was her unwavering faith, her deep understanding of God's purpose for her life, that emboldened her to act. And how did she reveal the hidden agenda of her enemy? Through writing. She penned a letter, exposing Haman's wicked plans and pleading for the protection of her people. Her written words became a powerful instrument for change, influencing the course of history and securing the future of her people.

Or consider Deborah, a judge and prophetess who led the Israelites to victory against the Canaanites. She was not only a woman of immense faith and courage but also a skilled orator and writer. Her words, whether spoken in a fiery sermon or penned on parchment, carried the weight of God's authority, inspiring her people to fight for their freedom and shaping the destiny of their nation.

And then there is Mary, the mother of Jesus, whose story is a testament to the power of faith and the enduring strength of a woman's heart. While her life may not have been filled with public acclaim, her written words, recorded in the book of Luke, carry a profound message of hope and redemption. Her Magnificat, a prayer of praise and anticipation, reverberates through the ages, capturing the essence of her deep faith and the anticipation of God's transformative power.

These women, and countless others throughout history, demonstrate the profound impact that women of faith can have on the world through their written words. Your words are not just a means of communication; they are a channel of God's grace, a vehicle for spreading His message, and a powerful tool for shaping the destiny of individuals and nations.

But how do you unlock the potential of your writing, allowing God to use you as a vessel for His message? It begins with a deep commitment to prayer and seeking God's guidance. Spend time in His presence, allowing Him to fill your heart with His wisdom and inspire your mind with His truth. As you open your heart to His promptings, He will guide your hand, revealing the stories He wants you to tell, the words He wants you to write, and the impact He wants you to make.

Journaling is another crucial tool in your arsenal. It provides a safe space to explore your thoughts and emotions, allowing you to document the journey of your faith. As you pour your heart onto the pages of your journal, you will unveil hidden insights, uncover the depths of your soul, and begin to understand the unique message that God has entrusted to you.

Beyond journaling, consider using writing as a means of spiritual exploration. Study the Bible, meditating on God's Word and allowing it to shape your understanding of His character, His plans, and His purpose for your life. The more you immerse yourself in His Word, the more your writing will become a conduit for His message, a powerful expression of His love and truth.

And as you write, be mindful of your audience. Who are you writing for? What message are you trying to convey? Remember, your words have the power to inspire, to challenge, to heal, to transform. Don't underestimate the impact your writing can have. Let your words be a source of light, a beacon of hope, a conduit for God's love and grace.

The enemy knows the power of written revelation. He knows that words can ignite hope, inspire faith, and empower individuals to break free from the shackles of fear and doubt.

That's why he will try to silence your voice, to discourage you from writing, to keep you locked in the chains of self-doubt and insecurity. But remember, you are not alone in this fight. The Lord is with you, empowering you with His strength and guiding you with His wisdom.

Embrace the power of written revelation. Allow God to use you as a vessel for His message, sharing your stories, your insights, your experiences, and your unique perspective on the world. Your writing has the potential to impact lives, to change destinies, and to leave a legacy of faith and inspiration that will resonate long after you are gone. Step into your calling, embrace your destiny, and let your words become a powerful force for good in the world. The world needs your voice, your stories, your truth. Let your writing become a testament to the power of God's love, a beacon of hope in a world that desperately needs it.

Shaping Destinies and Transforming Lives

The impact of words is a profound force, capable of shaping destinies and transforming lives. Words hold the power to inspire, to heal, to condemn, and to destroy. In the realm of prophetic writing, this power is magnified, for the words penned carry the weight of divine revelation, shaping the course of individuals and communities. Just as God spoke the world into existence with His words, so too can our words, when aligned with His spirit, create and change.

Imagine a sculptor, their hands deftly moving across a block of marble, chiseling away at the stone, revealing the masterpiece hidden within. The sculptor's tools are the words, and the marble is the life of the individual. With each stroke of the chisel, the words carve away at the limitations, the doubts, and the fears, revealing the beauty and potential that God has instilled within. Prophetic writing, when guided by the Holy Spirit, acts as this divine chisel, shaping the destiny of the individual and revealing the tapestry of their God-given purpose.

But with this immense power comes a tremendous responsibility. Words are not mere ink on paper or pixels on a screen; they are living entities, capable of impacting the world in profound ways. The responsibility of the prophetic writer is to wield this power with humility, integrity, and a deep reverence for the divine source of their message. They are entrusted with conveying the voice of God, the whispers of truth, and the guidance that leads individuals closer to their destiny.

This responsibility demands a constant and intimate connection with the Holy Spirit, an ongoing dialogue with the divine author of our lives. It is through this connection that the prophetic writer receives the words to write, the revelations to share, and the wisdom to navigate the delicate balance between clarity and accuracy. The words penned are not the writer's own; they are the words of God, channeled through the human vessel, imbued with the power of the divine.

Consider the words of the prophets in the Bible, words that echoed through time, shaping the course of history and leaving an indelible mark on humanity. Isaiah's words, "Comfort, comfort my people, says your God," offered solace and hope to a nation in turmoil. Jeremiah's words, "For I know the plans I have for you, declares the Lord, plans to prosper you and not to harm you, plans to give you hope and a future," ignited faith and instilled confidence in the midst of adversity. These words, imbued with divine inspiration, transformed lives, guided nations, and shaped the destiny of generations to come.

The power of words is evident in our everyday lives as well. Kind words can uplift and heal, while harsh words can wound and destroy. Words of encouragement can propel individuals towards their dreams, while words of criticism can dampen their spirits and hold them back. Words have the power to build or to break, to create or to destroy.

In the realm of prophetic writing, the responsibility to wield words with wisdom and grace is paramount. It requires a heart attuned to the voice of God, a mind disciplined to discern truth from falsehood, and a soul committed to serving the divine purpose of the message. It is not about personal glory or fame, but about obedience to the divine mandate, about becoming a conduit for God's truth to flow into the lives of others.

As you embark on your own journey of prophetic writing, remember the weight and the power of the words you pen. Seek guidance from the Holy Spirit, cultivate a deep connection with God, and write with a heart overflowing with love, compassion, and integrity. Embrace the responsibility that comes with wielding this divine power, and let your words become instruments of transformation, shaping destinies and transforming lives, one word at a time.

Uncovering Gods Plans for Your Life

Deep within the tapestry of your existence lies a divine blueprint, a master plan meticulously crafted by the Creator Himself. It's not a generic design, a one-size-fits-all template. No, this blueprint is uniquely tailored for you, a masterpiece that reflects your individual gifts, passions, and calling. It's a roadmap to a life brimming with purpose, fulfillment, and the profound joy of walking in alignment with God's will.

Imagine a master artist, painstakingly sketching out the intricate details of a breathtaking masterpiece. Each stroke, each shade, carefully chosen to bring forth a vision of beauty and brilliance. Just as this artist pours his soul into his creation, God, the ultimate Artist, has poured His love, His wisdom, and His divine intention into the tapestry of your life.

Zion's Blueprint blueprint isn't hidden away in a dusty attic, waiting to be discovered. It's woven into the very fabric of your being, pulsating with life, whispering secrets of your potential, and beckoning you to step into the destiny He has prepared for you. It's waiting for you to awaken to its presence, to unwrap its layers of revelation, and to embrace the extraordinary journey that awaits.

But this Zion's Blueprint isn't simply about a grand plan, a lofty goal to strive for. It's about the intimate journey of discovering who you are in Christ, of embracing your unique identity as a daughter of the King, and of embracing the strategies and assignments that God has specifically tailored for you.

The enemy, the one who seeks to steal, kill, and destroy, has often sought to silence the voices of women, to dim their lights and constrict their potential. But the Lord has a different plan, a plan of liberation, a plan of empowerment. He is calling you, dear sister, to step into your God-given authority, to rise above the limitations of the world and the whispers of doubt, and to embrace the extraordinary power that resides within you.

The divine blueprint is not just a roadmap; it's a treasure map. It's a guide to hidden treasures, to buried potential waiting to be unearthed, and to the profound joy that comes from living a life aligned with God's will. It's about understanding your unique gifts, recognizing your God-given talents, and stepping into the roles that only you can fulfill.

Picture a magnificent garden, bursting with vibrant flowers, each one a testament to the Creator's artistry. Just as each flower possesses a distinct beauty and purpose, so too do you, dear sister. You are not meant to be a generic bloom, blending into the background. You are meant to shine with your own radiant beauty, to blossom in the fullness of your potential, and to contribute your unique fragrance to the world.

This divine blueprint isn't just about external achievements; it's about an inward transformation, a spiritual awakening that begins in the secret place, the place of solitude and intimacy with God. It's about cultivating a deeper connection with the One who created you, seeking His wisdom and guidance in every aspect of your life, and surrendering to His will with a heart full of trust and obedience.

This journey of unveiling your divine blueprint is a lifelong adventure, a path of continuous growth and transformation.

It's a journey that will lead you through valleys and mountaintops, through trials and triumphs. But along the way, you will discover a strength you never knew you possessed, a resilience that defies the odds, and an unwavering faith that will sustain you through every storm.

As you embrace the strategies and assignments outlined in your divine blueprint, you will begin to experience the power and presence of God in ways you never imagined. You will witness the unfolding of His plan in your life, the manifestation of His glory in your every endeavor, and the transformation that takes place as you step into the destiny He has designed for you.

But this journey isn't a solo expedition; it's a shared journey, a symphony of faith, a chorus of voices rising up in unity and purpose. You are surrounded by a community of sisters, women who have embraced their divine blueprints, who have walked through the fire, and who are now standing alongside you, offering their support, their encouragement, Zion's Blueprint is yours.

So dear sister, as you embark on this extraordinary journey of unveiling your divine blueprint, remember that you are not alone. You are loved, you are cherished, and you are empowered by the very Creator of the universe. Embrace your God-given identity, step into the fullness of your potential, and let the world witness the beauty, the strength, and the brilliance of the woman you were created to be. The divine blueprint is yours, and your destiny awaits.

Unveiling Your GodGiven Potential

The journey toward fulfilling your destiny is not just a passive waiting game; it requires active engagement. God has meticulously crafted a unique blueprint for your life, weaving within it specific gifts and talents that are meant to shine brightly. You are not just a vessel to be filled; you are a masterpiece in progress, with God's fingerprint etched upon your very essence.

Imagine an intricate tapestry, each thread representing a distinct facet of your being. There's the silken thread of creativity, the sturdy thread of leadership, the delicate thread of compassion, and the vibrant thread of communication. All these threads, when woven together, create a masterpiece that reflects your unique calling and purpose.

To unveil this intricate tapestry, to understand the symphony of your gifts and talents, you must engage in a process of self-discovery. It's not about seeking validation or comparing yourself to others; it's about seeking God's perspective on who He created you to be.

Here are some practical steps you can take:

Seek God's Guidance: Prayer is the cornerstone of this journey. Take time to sit in the quiet presence of God, asking Him to reveal your gifts and talents. The Bible speaks of a hidden treasure that can be found only through seeking (Matthew 13:44). This hidden treasure is the knowledge of your own God-given potential.

Reflect on Your Past: As you look back on your life, identify moments when you felt a sense of fulfillment, joy, and deep satisfaction. What activities or situations ignited a passion within you? These experiences often offer clues to your inherent gifts.

Explore Your Interests: What subjects or hobbies draw you in? What activities leave you energized and inspired? These interests often point to your God-given talents. It's important to note that some of these interests may seem insignificant or frivolous to the world, but they can be significant in God's eyes.

Seek Feedback from Others: Ask trusted friends, family members, or mentors what they see as your strengths and areas of talent. Often, we are blind to our own gifts, but others can readily see them.

Pay Attention to Your Inner Voice: Pay attention to the promptings of your heart. There is a divine whisper within you, guiding you toward your destiny. As you listen, you'll start to discern the unique path that God has prepared for you.

Remember, it's not just about discovering your gifts and talents; it's about cultivating them.

Invest in Development: Once you identify your gifts, seek opportunities to develop them. This may involve taking classes, attending workshops, or engaging in activities that nurture your growth.

Embrace Challenges: Challenges are not setbacks; they are opportunities for growth. Don't shy away from stepping outside your comfort zone and taking on tasks that stretch your abilities.

Serve Others: Using your gifts and talents to serve others is a powerful way to refine and develop them. When we serve others, we unlock a deeper sense of purpose and fulfillment.

The journey of discovering your God-given potential is a lifelong endeavor. It's a journey of revelation, growth, and transformation. As you embrace the strategies and assignments outlined in this book, you will begin to see your life unfold in ways you could have never imagined.

The enemy wants to keep you bound, but God desires to set you free. He wants you to step into your destiny, wielding your gifts and talents as powerful tools for His kingdom.

Embrace this journey with courage, conviction, and unwavering faith. Your God-given potential is waiting to be unleashed.

Living in Harmony with Gods Will

Imagine a symphony, a masterpiece orchestrated by the divine conductor, with each note, each instrument playing its part in perfect harmony. This, dear sisters, is the power of alignment, living in resonance with God's will. It's not about forcing our will, but surrendering to His, allowing His divine blueprint to guide our every step.

The enemy desires to keep us off-key, playing discordant notes in the symphony of our lives. He throws distractions, temptations, and fear into the mix, hoping to drown out the beautiful melody of our true destiny. But God, the Master Composer, calls us to a life of exquisite harmony. He has given us specific strategies, assignments, and an intricate plan that will unlock the power within us and unleash our full potential.

Think of a skilled musician who carefully studies the sheet music, practices diligently, and refines their technique. They become attuned to the nuances of each note, the flow of the melody, and the intricate relationship between all the instruments. You too, my sisters, must diligently study the "sheet music" of God's Word, seeking His guidance through prayer, meditation, and His whispers to our hearts.

This "divine blueprint," as I like to call it, isn't a rigid set of rules but a vibrant tapestry of love, wisdom, and purpose. God doesn't simply want us to be passive participants in our lives. He desires us to be active collaborators, fully engaged in the symphony of His creation. He invites us to embrace our unique talents, gifts, and personalities, knowing that each one of us contributes to the grand masterpiece He is creating.

But the symphony isn't always smooth sailing. Sometimes, the music gets interrupted, the rhythm falters, and the harmony is threatened. Perhaps life throws unexpected challenges, doubt creeps in, or the enemy tempts us to stray from the melody. But God, the Master Composer, is ever-present, always ready to guide and support us. He provides us with the resources, strength, and courage to overcome these obstacles and stay on course.

Think of a pianist who encounters a particularly challenging passage in a piece. She might practice it over and over, seek guidance from her teacher, and even take a break when needed. Yet, she never gives up, knowing that with persistence and the right guidance, she can conquer the obstacle. We, too, dear sisters, must learn to navigate these challenging passages in our lives. We must seek God's wisdom, embrace His strength, and trust in His faithfulness to guide us through.

The journey of alignment is not always easy. There will be times when we feel lost, discouraged, or tempted to give up. But the beauty of it all is that we are not alone in this journey. God, our loving Father, is always by our side, ready to guide us, comfort us, and empower us. He is the source of our strength, the wellspring of our hope, and the architect of our destiny.

He invites us to step into the symphony of His creation, to play our part with passion, dedication, and unwavering faith. And as we align ourselves with His will, embracing His strategies and assignments, we will experience a profound transformation. We will be awakened to our true potential, experience an overflow of His presence, and leave a legacy of faith and impact on the world.

Embracing the Journey of Faith

Every woman's journey is unique, a tapestry woven with threads of triumphs and trials, victories and valleys. The path we tread is not always smooth; obstacles rise like towering mountains, casting long shadows of doubt and fear. Yet, within each challenge lies an opportunity for growth, a chance to lean into the strength and faithfulness of our God. He has not called us to a life devoid of hardship, but rather a journey where He is our steadfast companion, guiding us through the storms and empowering us to conquer every obstacle.

Remember the mighty woman of faith, Esther? Faced with a decree that threatened her people, she stepped forward with courage, trusting in the power of God to work through her. She chose to embrace her destiny, even when fear whispered its insidious doubts. Her story reminds us that God can use the most ordinary among us to accomplish extraordinary things.

Similarly, consider the apostle Paul, a man who faced countless trials, from imprisonment to persecution. Yet, in the midst of his struggles, he remained steadfast in his faith, proclaiming the gospel with unwavering boldness. His life stands as a testament to the enduring power of faith in the face of adversity.

These stories, and countless others throughout the scriptures, offer us a beacon of hope, a reminder that God is always with us, even in the darkest moments. He promises to equip us with everything we need to overcome any challenge, to stand firm against the winds of opposition.

This is the power of alignment, my sisters. It is the key to unlocking your destiny, fulfilling your purpose, and experiencing a symphony of joy and fulfillment in every area of your lives. So embrace the divine blueprint, listen to the music of His heart, and play your part with unwavering faith and a heart full of love. For you are not just notes in a melody, but integral parts of a masterpiece, a symphony orchestrated by the divine.

Living a Life of Meaning and Impact

The significance of purpose is the heart of our existence, the very essence of why we are here on earth. It's not just about existing; it's about living with intention, with a driving force that gives direction to our days, our choices, and our impact on the world around us. Just like an artist uses their unique skills to create a masterpiece, so too are we given gifts and talents by God, and our purpose is to use them to create a masterpiece, not just for our own satisfaction, but for the benefit of others. This is where the real joy, the real fulfillment, and the real impact come into play.

Imagine a symphony orchestra, each musician playing a unique instrument, contributing their unique sound to the overall piece. The conductor, with their understanding of the composition, guides each musician, blending their individual talents to create a harmonious and awe-inspiring performance. In the same way, God has a unique plan for each of us, a symphony He desires to play through our lives, using our individual talents and abilities to create something beautiful and impactful.

But the reality is, many women struggle to find their purpose, feeling lost in the complexities of life, unsure of their place in the grand scheme of things. They may feel overwhelmed by societal pressures, the demands of their daily lives, or the fear of failure, holding them back from pursuing their dreams and aspirations. They may feel like they are not making a difference, questioning their worth and their significance in the world.

This is where the power of faith, the revelation of God's will, and the embrace of His strategies come into play. The Holy

Spirit guides us, whispering in our hearts, revealing our unique calling and purpose. It's not about a generic "purpose" but about a specific one, a tailored plan designed just for you, a plan that aligns with your strengths, your passions, and your unique set of skills.

The question is, how do we discover this purpose? How do we unlock the potential within us, the unique tapestry of our lives that God has woven? It's about looking beyond the distractions of the world, silencing the noise, and finding the quiet space where God speaks. It's about delving into His Word, listening to His voice, and allowing the Holy Spirit to guide us towards our destiny.

The journey to finding your purpose is not always easy. It may involve stepping out of your comfort zone, confronting your fears, and embracing the unknown. It may mean letting go of old dreams and embracing new ones, trusting in God's plan even when it seems unclear or uncertain. But remember, God never asks us to do anything without equipping us with the tools and resources we need to succeed.

The first step is to identify your gifts and talents. What are you naturally good at? What comes easily to you? What are you passionate about? These are the building blocks of your purpose, the unique ingredients that will shape your contribution to the world.

For some, it may be a gift of leadership, a calling to guide and inspire others. For others, it may be a gift of creativity, a passion for using their artistic talents to communicate and connect with the world. For others, it may be a gift of compassion, a desire to serve and care for those in need.

The beauty of it all is that God can take even the most seemingly ordinary abilities and use them to create extraordinary impact. Think about the everyday things we often take for granted: a teacher who patiently inspires young minds, a nurse who tenderly cares for the sick, a mother who lovingly nurtures her children. These are not grand, flamboyant acts, but they are acts of purpose, acts that touch lives, and leave a lasting mark on the world.

As you begin to identify your gifts and talents, it's important to seek God's guidance. Ask Him to reveal His specific plan for your life, the unique role He has designed for you to play. He will show you, step by step, how to use your gifts to make a difference, to create a ripple effect that touches countless lives.

Don't be afraid to step out of your comfort zone. Embrace the challenges that come your way. Remember, God has not called us to mediocrity, but to greatness. He has given us the potential to live lives filled with purpose, impact, and significance. He has given us the power to shape our world for good.

Imagine the impact we could have if each of us embraced our unique calling. If we used our gifts and talents to build up the world, to heal the brokenhearted, to inspire hope, to spread love and compassion. The world would be a very different place.

The call to purpose is a call to action, a call to step into our God-given identity and live out the plan He has for us. It's not just about finding a job, a career, or a passion. It's about discovering our true selves, the people God created us to be, and living out that purpose with unwavering faith and bold determination.

So, sister, embrace the journey. Discover your purpose. Embrace the strategies and assignments God has given you.

And let your life be a masterpiece, a symphony of love, light, and impact, resonating through the ages. Your life matters, your story has meaning, and your impact will be felt for generations to come. This is the significance of purpose - living a life that makes a difference, a life that leaves a legacy of faith, hope, and love, a life that echoes the love of God and inspires others to live lives of purpose as well.

Experiencing a Greater Anointing

The transformation of faith is a journey that often involves unexpected twists and turns. It's like a river, meandering through valleys and cascading over waterfalls, continually shaping and reshaping its course. As women embrace their destiny and align their lives with God's will, they embark on a transformative journey that unlocks a greater anointing and power within them.

Imagine a simple clay pot, plain and unremarkable. It holds no particular value or significance, just an empty vessel waiting to be filled. But what happens when that pot is placed in the hands of a skilled potter? The potter's touch transforms the clay, molding it into a beautiful, intricate design. Each stroke of the potter's hand unveils a hidden potential, revealing the artistry that lies within.

Similarly, our lives are like vessels, waiting to be shaped by the Master Potter. As we surrender to His guidance and allow Him to work in us, we experience a profound transformation. Our faith is refined, our understanding deepened, and our hearts are filled with an anointing that empowers us to live out our destiny.

This transformation isn't a singular event; it's a continuous process. It's about aligning ourselves with God's will, seeking His guidance, and allowing His Spirit to mold us into the people He intended us to be. It's about embracing the challenges and setbacks as opportunities for growth, trusting that God is working all things together for our good.

Think of it as a journey into the unknown, a pilgrimage to a sacred land. We don't always know the path ahead, but we trust that God is our faithful guide, leading us through every trial and triumph. He equips us with the strength and resilience we need to overcome obstacles and emerge stronger than before.

As we journey deeper into God's presence, our faith is tested and refined. We encounter situations that challenge our beliefs, forcing us to confront our fears and doubts. Yet, through these trials, God reveals His faithfulness and strengthens our trust in Him. We learn to discern His voice amidst the noise of the world, relying on His wisdom to guide our decisions.

This transformative process often begins in the secret place, where we cultivate a deeper relationship with God through prayer, meditation, and the study of His Word. It's in these moments of solitude and intimacy that we receive divine revelations, gain clarity on our purpose, and experience a renewed sense of hope and direction.

As we immerse ourselves in God's Word, we discover truths that shape our understanding and transform our hearts. The scriptures become a lamp unto our feet, illuminating the path ahead and guiding us toward a greater purpose. We begin to see women as more than just ordinary individuals; we realize they are vessels chosen by God to carry His presence and influence the world around us and to manifest Zion in the earth.

Through consistent prayer, we establish a powerful connection with God. Our prayers become a lifeline, a conduit through which we communicate our desires, anxieties, and praises. In the quiet moments of prayer, we experience the power of God's presence, receiving guidance, comfort, and strength to face the challenges ahead.

This transformation of faith isn't about striving to reach some unattainable level of perfection. It's about embracing the process, recognizing that we are still works in progress, and trusting God to complete the work He has started in us. It's about acknowledging our limitations and seeking His strength to overcome our weaknesses.

Daughters as you step into our destiny and live in alignment with God's will, we experience an overflow of His presence. His power begins to manifest in our lives, impacting not only our personal lives but also our relationships, our careers, and our influence on others. We become beacons of hope, shining His light into the world, and impacting lives in ways we never imagined.

Imagine a small seed, buried deep within the soil, seemingly insignificant and powerless. But within that seed lies the potential for a mighty oak tree, reaching high into the heavens, providing shade and shelter to all who seek it.

Our lives are like those seeds. We may feel small and insignificant, but within us lies the potential to blossom into something beautiful and powerful. As we embrace our destiny and allow God to work in us, we become instruments of His power, making a difference in the world.

This journey of faith is not a sprint; it's a marathon. There will be moments of joy and triumph, as well as periods of struggle and doubt. But through it all, God is faithful. He never leaves our side, and He never stops working in us. He desires to see us flourish, to fulfill our destiny, and to make a lasting impact on the world.

So, embrace the journey, embrace the transformation, and embrace the destiny God has for you. Let His presence flow through you, empowering you to live a life of purpose, impact, and significance. Your life is a masterpiece in the making, and God is the artist who is shaping it into a beautiful and powerful work of art.

Manifesting His Glory and Power

The overflow of God's presence is like a mighty river, a current of divine power that sweeps through our lives, transforming everything it touches. It's a surge of grace, a waterfall of love, and an undeniable manifestation of His glory. As we align ourselves with God's will, step into our destinies, and embrace the strategies He has given us, the doors to this overflow swing wide open. Imagine a mighty, roaring waterfall, cascading down into a pool of vibrant turquoise water, its power and energy palpable. That's what the overflow of God's presence feels like – a surge of divine power that washes over us, carrying us into deeper depths of His love.

It's not just about personal growth; it's about impacting our surroundings, leaving ripples that reverberate through generations. We are vessels designed to carry God's presence, and when we step into that purpose, we become conduits of His power, sharing His love with the world. Think of a humble clay pot, ordinary in its appearance. But when filled with precious oil, its significance transforms. The vessel itself is not the source of the oil, but it carries it, distributing its fragrance and light. Similarly, we are not the source of God's power, but when His presence flows through us, we become instruments of change, transforming our lives and the lives of those around us.

The key to unlocking this overflow lies in our obedience. It's about being willing to surrender our own plans and desires, allowing God to lead us down the path He has designed for us. It's about trusting His voice, even when it leads us into unfamiliar territory. It's about saying "yes" to His will, even when it means stepping out of our comfort zones and into the unknown. Remember the story of Gideon, a humble farmer who was chosen to lead the Israelites against the Midianites. He was hesitant, doubting his own ability. But God assured him, "I will be with you," and Gideon, in faith, embraced the challenge. His obedience, his trust in God's promise, led to an incredible victory.

This victory wasn't just about military triumph; it was about a manifestation of God's power. The presence of God flowed through Gideon, empowering him to lead his people to victory, and his life became a testament to God's faithfulness. In the same way, when we embrace our destinies and align with God's will, we become instruments of His power, witnessing miracles, seeing breakthroughs, and experiencing a transformation that extends beyond ourselves.

The overflow of God's presence is not a passive experience. It's an active pursuit, a journey of faith and obedience. It requires us to step out of our comfort zones, embrace challenges, and trust in His guidance. It's about living with intentionality, seeking His will in every decision, and walking in the power of His Spirit. Imagine a riverbed that is dry and barren. But as the river starts to flow, it brings life and nourishment to the surrounding land, transforming the desolate landscape into a vibrant oasis. Our lives are similar. When we embrace our destinies and allow God's presence to flow through us, we bring life and transformation to the world around us.

This overflow isn't limited to individual experiences. It's a force that ripples outward, impacting our families, communities, and even the nations. As we live out our destinies, our impact spreads, igniting a chain reaction of positive change. Imagine a seed dropped into fertile soil. It doesn't just grow into a single plant; it multiplies, producing more seeds that sprout and bloom, creating a field of life.

That's what happens when we tap into the overflow of God's presence. We become agents of change, spreading His love and transforming our world.

The overflow of God's presence is a beautiful and powerful force. It's a manifestation of His love, a demonstration of His power, and a testament to His faithfulness. When we embrace our destinies, align with His will, and step into the purpose He has for us, we become conduits of this overflow, transforming our lives and impacting the world around us. It's a journey of faith, a dance of obedience, and a testament to the boundless love and power of our Heavenly Father. As you walk into the next chapter of your life, remember this: you are designed to carry His presence, to be a vessel of His love, and to witness His glory unfolding in your life and through you. Embrace your destiny. Step into the overflow. Let His power transform your world.

Leaving a Lasting Legacy of Faith and Impact

The journey of unlocking your destiny and increasing God's presence is a transformative one, a path illuminated by faith and fueled by the divine power that resides within you. It is a journey of awakening, where you shed the layers of doubt and fear, embracing the true power and purpose that God has bestowed upon you. As you step into this journey, you become a beacon of light, radiating God's love and grace, impacting the world in ways you never imagined.

Remember the vision you received, the glimpses into the divine plan for your life. This vision is not a mere dream, but a divine blueprint, a tapestry woven by the hand of God. It is a roadmap that guides you towards your God-given potential, a call to embrace your true identity and step into the fullness of your destiny.

This journey is not a solitary endeavor. God walks beside you, His presence a constant source of strength, guidance, and comfort. It is a journey of surrendering to His will, relinquishing your own desires and plans, and trusting in His perfect design. This surrender is not a sign of weakness but a testament to your faith, a profound trust in the power and love of a God who knows you better than you know yourself.

As you align your life with His will, you will experience a greater anointing, a divine power flowing through you, transforming your life and empowering you to impact your world. It is in the secret place of intimacy with God, where you seek His guidance through prayer, meditation, and His Word, that you tap into this reservoir of power. It is in the act of writing, journaling, and releasing prophetic messages that you unlock the hidden depths of revelation, aligning your heart and mind with the divine plan.

Every word you write, every message you share, carries the potential to transform lives and shape destinies. Your writing is a powerful tool, a divine weapon wielded for the advancement of God's Kingdom. It is a legacy that transcends time, a testament to the power of His Word and the impact of a life lived in alignment with His purpose.

You are called to leave a lasting legacy of faith and impact on the world. To do so, you must embrace your God-given potential, the unique gifts and talents He has bestowed upon you. These gifts are not mere talents but spiritual gifts, tools for building His kingdom, for advancing His purposes on earth. Embrace these gifts, develop them, and use them to serve others, to shine the light of Christ into the darkness of the world.

Your life is not merely a story of personal transformation but a story that inspires and empowers others. It is a story of faith, of courage, of resilience, of overcoming obstacles and achieving victory through God's grace. Share your story, let your light shine, and inspire others to embrace their own destinies and unlock the fullness of God's presence in their lives.

This is the journey you are called to embark on, a journey of awakening, of transformation, of impact. It is a journey that starts with a single step, a commitment to seek God's will and live in alignment with His purpose. It is a journey that will lead you to a life of significance, a life that leaves a lasting legacy of faith and impact on the world.

Remember, you are not alone. God is with you, guiding you, empowering you, and equipping you for the journey ahead.

Embrace your destiny, walk boldly in your God-given identity, and allow the power of His presence to transform your life and impact the world around you.

Let your life be a testament to His love, a beacon of hope and inspiration for generations to come. Your journey has begun, and the possibilities are endless. Let your light shine.

Embracing a Lifetime of Growth and Purpose

The journey of faith is not a destination, but a continuous exploration, a lifelong pursuit of growth and purpose. Just as a seed planted in the earth doesn't simply sprout and then stop growing, so too our faith journeys are meant to blossom and bear fruit throughout our lives. We are called to be women of constant transformation, constantly evolving into the image of Christ, the ultimate embodiment of love, grace, and truth.

This journey, however, isn't about a singular destination. It's about embracing the process, the constant unveiling of God's plans, the intricate tapestry of His will woven into the fabric of our lives. There will be seasons of growth, periods of testing, and moments of glorious breakthrough. And within each stage, we are meant to learn, to refine, and to become more like the image of our Creator.

Just as a sculptor shapes clay with delicate strokes, refining and molding it into a masterpiece, God works in our lives, refining our character, shaping our desires, and molding us into instruments of His purpose. We may not always understand the process, or see the big picture, but we are called to trust, to lean into His guidance, and to allow Him to shape us into the women He created us to be.

Imagine a potter, carefully crafting each piece with meticulous precision, shaping the clay into a vessel of beauty. In the same way, God works with us, shaping our personalities, our passions, and our desires. We are His masterpieces, uniquely crafted and designed for a specific purpose, with a specific role to play in His unfolding plan.

The beauty of this journey is that it's never truly over. It's a continuous unfolding, a constant revelation of His purpose and plan. And as we walk in faith, seeking His direction, He continues to open doors, reveal opportunities, and empower us to step into the fullness of our destinies.

Imagine, for instance, a young woman, perhaps struggling to discern her calling. She may feel lost, unsure of her path, and questioning her abilities. But as she steps into the secret place of prayer, seeking God's guidance, she discovers a hidden talent, a passion for helping others. This becomes the catalyst for her journey, the starting point of her transformation, as she embraces the gifts God has given her and steps into her God-given purpose.

This journey isn't about becoming perfect, but about becoming more like Christ, embracing His grace and allowing Him to work within us. It's about shedding old patterns, breaking free from the chains of fear and doubt, and embracing the freedom that comes from living in alignment with God's will.

As we continue to grow, we may face challenges and setbacks. But God promises that He will always be with us, a constant source of strength, guidance, and encouragement. The journey of faith is never easy, but it is always worth it.

You are called to be women of courage, women who embrace the journey, who trust in His promises, and who walk in faith, knowing that He has a divine plan for each of our lives. You are daughters of the King, chosen and empowered to make a difference in the world. And as we step into our destinies, we become living testaments to His love and His grace.

Remember, the journey is not a straight line, but a winding path, with twists and turns, unexpected detours, and breathtaking views. And through it all, God will be our constant guide, leading you, nurturing you, and ultimately shaping you into the women He created you to be.

This is a journey of faith, a lifelong pursuit of purpose, a testament to the transforming power of God. Embrace it, trust it, and let your life become a living reflection of His glory.

Walking in Boldness and Confidence

So, sisters, you stand on the precipice of your destinies, embrace the audacity of faith! Cast aside the whispers of doubt and fear and instead, walk with an unwavering confidence in the power of God's Word and His promises for your lives. You have been called to greatness! To a life that radiates the glory of God, leaving an undeniable mark on this world.

You are daughters of the Most High, and He has equipped you with the strength, wisdom, and authority to navigate the challenges that lie ahead. It's time to step into the fullness of your identity, the one He has so beautifully crafted for you. Let the world see the brilliance of your God-given purpose reflected in your lives.

Remember the promises He's made to you! His Word is alive and active, a guiding light in the darkest of nights. It's the compass that will keep you on course, the anchor that will hold you steady in the storms of life. Let the promises of His Word fuel your courage, empower your steps, and ignite the fire of passion within your hearts.

As you embrace the transformative power of writing and allow the pen to become an instrument of revelation, you will unveil the depths of your spiritual potential. You will see your destinies unfolding before your very eyes, divinely orchestrated by the hands of our Creator. Let the words you write be inspired by His Word, reflecting the beauty of His character and the power of His love. Let them become the catalyst for change, not only in your own lives but in the lives of others.

Embrace the journey, sisters! It won't always be easy, but with God by your side, you can conquer every obstacle, navigate every storm, and emerge stronger than ever before. His grace is sufficient, His strength is made perfect in our weakness, and His love is an unyielding force that will carry you through every challenge.

Don't let the world dictate your worth. Don't let its doubts and limitations define your potential. Instead, let the truth of God's Word be your compass, His love your strength, and His grace your shield. Step into the fullness of your destiny with boldness and confidence, knowing that you are loved, cherished, and empowered by the Almighty. You are a chosen vessel, uniquely crafted to fulfill His purpose and leave a lasting legacy that echoes throughout the ages.

Remember, sisters, the journey is not about perfection but about progress. It's about embracing the process, learning from your mistakes, and growing closer to God with each passing day. Don't be afraid to stumble, to fall, or to ask for help. The Lord is always there, ready to lift you up, restore you, and guide you back onto the path He has ordained for your lives.

So, let walk with courage, with confidence, and with a deep knowing that you are not alone. Lean into the strength of your God, allowing His power to flow through you, transforming you into the women He has always envisioned you to be. You are daughters of the King, and your destiny is intertwined with His glory! Rise to the occasion, embrace your call, and shine brightly in the world for His sake!
Love You And Honor You
Dr. Phil Spears Th.d DD.

Acknowledgments

To the women who have dared to dream, to those who have fought for their freedom, and to those who continue to rise in faith and purpose, this book is for you. Your courage inspires me, your struggles strengthen me, and your triumphs fill me with hope. Thank you for being the embodiment of God's love and grace in this world.

I am deeply grateful to my staff, at Sheba International Churches for there unwavering support and encouragement throughout this journey. Your love, patience, and understanding have been a constant source of strength and inspiration.

To my children, Phil Spears Jr, Alyssie Spears, Dawson Spears, and my Bug your laughter and love brings joy to my heart. You remind me daily of the precious gift of family and the importance of living a life filled with purpose.

To my fellow believers, your prayers and support have been a powerful force in my life. I am blessed to walk this path with you, and I am eternally grateful for your love and friendship.

I would also like to acknowledge the dedicated team at [Publisher's name] for their unwavering belief in this message and for their tireless efforts in bringing this book to fruition. Your commitment to excellence is truly inspiring.

Finally, to the Lord Jesus Christ, my Savior and my Lord, thank you for your endless love, grace, and guidance. You are my everything, and I am eternally grateful for the privilege of serving you.

Appendix

This book is intended as a starting point for your own journey of discovery. It is not meant to be an exhaustive resource, but rather a springboard for your own exploration of God's Word and His will for your life. For further study and insight, I recommend the following resources:

The Bible: The ultimate source of truth and guidance for all believers.
Christian Classics: Works by renowned Christian authors, such as C.S. Lewis, Augustine of Hippo, and John Piper.
Prophetic Ministries: Seek out prophetic ministries that are led by the Holy Spirit and that align with the teachings of God's Word.
Online Resources: There are numerous websites and online resources dedicated to women's ministry, spiritual growth, and prophetic understanding.
www.shebachurches.com

Glossary

Discernment: The ability to distinguish between truth and error, right and wrong, good and evil.

Destiny: The predetermined course of events that God has planned for your life.

Prophetic: Relating to the utterance or interpretation of divine revelation.

Revelation: The unveiling or disclosure of divine truth.

Secret Place: A time and place where you can draw near to God in prayer, meditation, and solitude.

Spiritual Vision: The ability to see beyond the natural realm and perceive God's truth and purpose.

Strategies and Assignments: Specific plans and tasks that God has given you to fulfill your destiny.

Veil of Deception: The enemy's tactics used to deceive and hinder women, including fear, doubt, and manipulation.

References

This book incorporates various scriptural references, including but not limited to the following passages:

Isaiah 55:10-11
Jeremiah 29:11
Psalm 23
Proverbs 3:5-6
Ephesians 2:10
Galatians 5:1
Philippians 4:6-7
1 Thessalonians 5:16-18
1 Peter 2:9

Author Biography

Dr. Phil Spears is a Christian Evangelist, Prophetic Speaker, and writer. He is passionate about sharing the message of hope and freedom found in Christ, particularly among men and women. Through his ministry, he encourages men and women to discover their God-given identity and purpose, to embrace their spiritual authority, and to live a life of impact and significance.

Dr, Phil Spears is a gifted storyteller and his passion for writing stems from a deep desire to inspire and empower others. He is the author of several books and articles on faith, empowerment, and prophetic ministry. He is also a sought-after speaker at conferences, retreats, and events worldwide.

Dr, Phil Spears resides in Knoxville, Tn He is an active member of Sheba International Churches and is currently serving as its Presiding Prelate.

www.ingramcontent.com/pod-product-compliance
Lightning Source LLC
Chambersburg PA
CBHW070242220526
45465CB00004B/1486